INBOUND

ORGANIZATION

INBOUND

ORGANIZATION

How to Build and Strengthen
Your Company's Future
Using **Inbound** Principles

DAN TYRE | TODD HOCKENBERRY

WILEY

*To business owners working hard every day
to build a solution, product, or service that buyers love*

*To people working in those businesses trying their best
to help*

*To the inbound believers at HubSpot,
their partners, and their customers and users*

To our families, who allowed us to share this book with you

Contents

Foreword

If you ask people who know us where Dharmesh and I got the idea to start HubSpot, they'll probably tell you our starting point was the shifting balance of power between buyers and sellers.

They wouldn't be wrong. The vendor-client relationship has changed, and it has permanently altered how we do business. But the real story is much bigger than that.

We didn't start HubSpot because we thought only marketing was changing. We started HubSpot because we saw technology changing the world faster than ever before, and we wanted to democratize that change so small businesses could unlock their potential and grow.

The buyer-seller relationship is just one example of the dozens of ways technology impacts the way we do business. It all started when people began taking the Internet (and the free flow of information it enabled) seriously, around the early 1990s. The rise of the Internet empowered people to educate themselves, share insights, and share feedback, and ultimately it allowed us to demand more for ourselves.

If all of this sounds painfully obvious, that's just a testament to how thoroughly the Internet has changed our expectations of the people we do business with. But back in 1990, you might not have seen any of this coming.

Unless you're Rick Levine, Christopher Locke, Doc Searls, or David Weinberger. In 2000, they penned the ahead-of-its-time book *The Cluetrain Manifesto: The End of Business as Usual,* which accurately predicted the Internet's impact on organizations' interactions with their employees and marketplace.

I first read the manifesto when I was working for Ray Ozzie at Groove Networks, a legendary software entrepreneur who became CTO of Microsoft after they acquired Groove. He believed these four authors were seeing into the future, and he built Groove to help organizations run the way the *Cluetrain Manifesto* authors thought they should.

The authors had one message they wanted businesses to hear, loud and clear: "We are not seats or eyeballs or end users or consumers. We are human beings—and our reach exceeds your grasp."

In other words, this is the core philosophy HubSpot was founded upon: treat everybody like they're a human or become obsolete. We call it "inbound."

The book begins with 95 theses, a play on Martin Luther's 95 theses that he nailed to a church door in Germany. Most of these theses still ring true today and in many ways describe a world we still haven't reached. Here are some of my favorites:

Markets are conversations.

Markets consist of human beings, not demographic sectors.

Conversations among human beings sound human. They are conducted in a human voice.

Whether delivering information, opinions, perspectives, dissenting arguments, or humorous asides, the human voice is typically open, natural, and uncontrived.

People recognize each other as such from the sound of this voice.

The Internet is enabling conversations among human beings that were simply not possible in the era of mass media.

In both internetworked markets and among intranet-worked employees, people are speaking to each other in a powerful new way.

These networked conversations are enabling powerful new forms of social organization and knowledge exchange to emerge.

As a result, markets are getting smarter, more informed, more organized. Participation in a networked market changes people fundamentally.

When Dharmesh and I founded HubSpot, we baked these principles into the core of our product and go-to-market strategy. We wanted to disrupt the way companies engage with their markets, and we've always been committed to helping our prospects rather than treating them like lines on a P&L.

We didn't stop with the product, though. The *Cluetrain Manifesto* isn't just about companies and their markets—it touches every aspect of how organizations do business, externally and internally. Companies that can't recognize what their constituents want won't be able to compete and will go away.

Why?

First, the Internet drastically changed the power dynamic between companies and their employees.

In the pre-Internet age, career development went something like this: People would graduate high school or college, take a job, and work their way up the corporate ladder. Employees tended to stay with the same company for many years, and frontline workers didn't have much influence in decision making.

Most organizations were rigidly hierarchical and designed to keep leverage in the employer's hands. Companies placed their key decision makers at the top of a pyramid, and everyone below fed them information.

Before the Internet, this was the most efficient way for companies to operate. Individual frontline employees worked on tiny slices of the company, and they had little influence or knowledge that could contribute to major decisions.

So people hoarded information. Knowing something nobody else did gave you power, and was the quickest way to get access to higher-ups and advance your career. What data you did possess was difficult to quickly disseminate and was usually reserved for the higher-ups' ears only. As a result, only people with formal authority—the CEO and other C-level actors—had enough context to make decisions.

Today, it would be laughable for someone to stay at the same company their entire career. Junior employees provide input on strategic decisions all the time. You'd be hard-pressed to find a company where a CEO knows more about what's happening on the ground than her frontline employees. And if a company treats its employees like cogs in a machine, you'd better believe people will find out—fast.

Second, the Internet drastically changed the power dynamic between companies and their customers.

Just as it was hard for information to spread within a company, there were no channels like Yelp where customers treated badly could share their stories. So companies could strong-arm buyers into deals with bad terms and use interruptive sales and marketing tactics without fear of backlash.

Before information was so readily available online, buyers also had to rely 100% on what sellers said about their products. There were no places that aggregated product information or customer feedback, so buyers either had to rely on their personal networks for recommendations or take companies at their word.

Today, there are thousands of review aggregation sites, companies are extremely transparent about their pricing, and every company has a features listing web page.

There is no room for the old way of doing things anymore. Information within and among companies is ubiquitous. People demand far more from their employers and vendors because they can. And that's better for everyone.

When knowledge is concentrated in the hands of a small group of people and nothing forces those with power to take care of those without, things get worse. When the same people call all the shots, companies can quickly fall into a rut because they lack diversity of thought. When the market doesn't punish companies for not treating their employees and customers well, they have no financial incentive to do so.

We used to live in an outbound world. Players who traditionally held power and information—employers, vendors, bosses—could pretty much dictate the terms of their relationships with their constituents. But that's not the case anymore.

Today, we're living in an inbound world. People only give their time, money, and attention to institutions and people that delight them. Inbound marketing, sales, and customer success is just part of that equation—it's how organizations should talk to their marketplace.

Within an organization, inbound is just as important. As Dan and Todd write in this book, to do inbound, you have to be inbound. That means treating your employees like the valuable contributors they are, not seat-fillers who are expendable. That means inverting the pyramid of power so your frontline employees, who have the best information on how your prospects and customers behave, can tell their managers, and their manager's managers, what they're seeing and how it should affect your company's future.

At HubSpot, that also means openly sharing information about our market and our business so everyone from our president to a new hire can make good decisions. That means asking our customers and partners for feedback—and actually listening to it—so we can get better and avoid being blindsided by irrelevance.

The companies that keep their employees in the dark, pummel their prospects into buying, and squeeze every last drop of value from their customers without giving anything in return simply can't compete. There's nowhere to hide.

The *Cluetrain Manifesto* guys knew this all the way back in 2000. And 18 years later, the marketplace is just starting to catch up.

For example: When we first started HubSpot, we didn't have a formal organizational chart, and I was adamant about never having one. We sat down one day to draw a "shadow" organizational chart that mapped influence, and we found that some of the most influential people weren't formally imbued with a great deal of power. That's how we believe it should be—influence and power aren't reserved for those who sit at the top of a formal hierarchy.

In 2007, though, our employees weren't ready for such a radical shift—an organization without job titles or chains of command you could track on paper. So we created a job title structure and an organizational chart. The social pressures associated with explaining to your Uncle Ted what you do for a living when you go home for the holidays have not gone away entirely—and certainly existed in full force when we founded the company almost 12 years ago.

So we came up with other ways to ensure frontline employees are empowered. We have an internal wiki where all our financials, slides from executive team meetings, details on new initiatives, and postmortems of experiments are published for the whole company to see. We created a Culture Code very early on so we could be very deliberate about the kind of workplace we wanted to be. We publish documents outlining each department's high-level strategy and plays for the year. We ask our frontline employees to pitch to us all year round so we don't get trapped in our executive ivory tower, and hold formal open calls for ideas so everyone has a chance to speak.

This is the direction we're all heading in. Eventually, you'll see more and more businesses where power is decentralized and no single individual wields a rubber stamp. This is the natural progression of things, and whether we get there in 15 years or 50, we are going to see organizations flatten more and more, as people tire of hierarchies and power structures. And once more, organizations that cannot adapt will disappear.

It's getting harder and harder to compete and get your company off the ground. When Dharmesh and I founded HubSpot, there were approximately 30 other competitors in our space. Today, there are over 5,000. It's getting easier and easier to start a company, and harder and harder to scale it up—the web giveth, and the Internet taketh away. To survive in this market, you have to get every piece of your organization right.

Great employees are drawn to a strong culture and a worthy mission—people don't want to work for companies where the end goal is nothing loftier than making two more cents per share this quarter. Treating your customers well means they'll spread the good word to their networks. Giving your partners the tools to succeed and flourish will lead to a long and healthy relationship, and guard against your competition.

Ultimately, it's pretty simple—do the right thing by your constituents, and they'll stick around. Information is everywhere. Word of mouth means everything. You can't get away with treating any of your constituents poorly anymore.

If you're not there yet, you're in luck. We're on the cusp of a seismic shift, and because you're reading this book, you get to be the first to learn how to move your business ahead, and build an organization to be inbound, inside and out.

When information is ubiquitous, we all do better. When everyone understands the big picture, they can figure out how to move the needle in the little universe of their job. It's not just Dharmesh and I sitting in a room making decisions. Everyone can learn a little more each day and improve their decision making and increase their impact. And eventually, the virtuous effects of this openness and idea sharing ripples all the way back up to the top of the organization.

The sooner a business can figure this out, the bigger of an advantage they will have in today's market. There's no guarantee that practicing inbound will lead to success—no one can guarantee that. But it's a certainty that without being inbound, an organization will get left behind. Don't let it happen to you. We can all do better and be better.

—Brian Halligan
CEO and Chairman, HubSpot

Preface

Free digital goods, the sharing economy, intangibles, and changes in our relationships have already had big effects on our well-being. They also call for new organizational structures, new skills, new institutions, and perhaps even a reassessment of some of our values.

—Erik Brynjolfsson and Andrew McAfee[1]

Who Needs to Be an Inbound Organization?

- Are you a senior executive thinking about growing your business and achieving competitive advantage?
- Are you an entrepreneur, business owner, or startup looking to scale?
- Are you a manager or team leader looking for a new approach that will position your organization to succeed?
- Are you a marketing, sales, or service manager looking for the best way to empower your team?
- Are you a CMO, CRO, or SVP in a large organization and wonder why your sales and marketing efforts seem to generate fewer and fewer net new sales with the same or even increased spending?
- Do you find it hard to create product or service differentiation in the age of abundant buyer options?
- Are you experiencing increased competition and decreased customer loyalty?
- Are you a young professional trying to decide what kind of company you want to work with to start and grow your career?

If you said yes to any of these questions, the ideas of *Inbound Organization* are for you.

This book is for the millions of companies around the world that may be struggling with building engagement with their customers, prospects, and a wide audience and are wondering why it gets harder and harder each year to grow revenue and build enduring customer relationships.

It is for the leaders of companies that struggle to build competitive advantage and have tried various marketing and sales tactics to no avail.

It is for:

Connie, the CEO and owner of a regulatory consulting firm, who needs to figure out how to get their compliance consultants more engaged with existing clients and prospects.

Wayne, the owner of a small capital equipment manufacturing company, who wants to drive new leads in new markets, is spending money with a marketing agency focusing on Google Adwords but is not getting any leads, and is trying to attract skilled workers in a tight labor market.

Kari, the owner of restaurants, manufacturing, and distribution companies, who needs to drive a consistent flow of leads to his distribution and manufacturing businesses, find enough opportunities to grow in a shrinking market sector, and align his team to changing market demands. He also needs to figure out how to get diners into his restaurants.

Paul, who runs marketing for a large manufacturing company that has a dominant market share in one product line but is struggling to grow other product lines, and who is fighting with his IT and sales departments, which are blocking his path to more online marketing investments.

Katie, who graduated from a local community college, is launching her first software company startup offering a recruiting app for seasonal workers, and needs to reach her target audience and generate her first hundred customers in the next 18 months.

And Larry, who wonders why he can't get prospects on the phone, why his cold calls and visits are only successful a small percentage of the time, and who needs to build a revenue-generation model for a future when he will not be a part of the business.

What This Book Is and Is Not

This book is about the principles, ideas, and tactics we see people successfully adopt that transform organizations into strong, enduring customer-centric businesses that are adept at building relationships that create competitive advantage. An inbound-focused business creates an amazing culture that treats employees and customers like human beings.

This book reveals the beliefs, principles, and strategies of these successful inbound organizations so that you can transform your organization into one too.

The book is intended to help leaders apply inbound practices across an organization and instill a new, holistic way of thinking about the entire business. This book is not just about marketing or sales, but how all departments fit together to deliver what buyers want today while creating a culture that fosters sustained success.

This book provides insights into building an organization that creates relationships with buyers, employees, partners—with anyone in your business's ecosystem—to establish a competitive advantage and increase brand recognition, conversion rates, and market share—whatever your industry.

To *do* inbound, you must *be* inbound.

This isn't a book about how to market and sell your product or service but rather it's about building an organization that has the people, culture, and strategies in place to succeed in the age of buyer control. An organization that wakes up every day focusing on making sure all of the people it touches are successful.

In other words, to be inbound.

Why We Wrote This Book

We have been involved in the inbound world for nearly a decade, and it has been fascinating to see the impact of inbound thinking on businesses worldwide. Starting with marketing and then moving to sales, the powerful concepts surrounding the inbound movement have morphed into a revolution of business transformation that has had a demonstrable impact on hundreds of thousands of companies and millions of people.

We are in the middle of a dramatic shift of the fundamental aspects of how companies create cultures, how businesses scale, how buyers purchase, and how businesses engage in meaningful conversations and lasting relationships with their customers. The next decade will only accelerate these changes. Companies who align their vision, philosophy, processes, systems, and tools with the way buyers think, learn, discover, and purchase will have a huge advantage.

Rather than only update a business plan, organizations must adjust their total mindset and establish a strategic foundation to succeed.

This book shows leaders how to build their company's future around inbound principles and create the new organizational foundations necessary to deal with the ongoing changes in buyer behavior.

This book will illustrate why and how the inbound customer experience conversation must take place in the boardrooms of companies, must be on the desks of founders, entrepreneurs, business leaders, consultants, advisors, and in the mind of anyone who is responsible for leading a team, a small business, or an enterprise into the future.

The fundamental premise behind being an inbound organization is simple: everyone in the organization must consider how their role specifically influences the customer journey to enhance the customer experience—hence the need for organizational leadership to focus on becoming an inbound organization.

The way most businesses are structured today is not conducive to building complete and extraordinary employee, partner, and customer relationships.

This book will address the gap in understanding and give business owners a road map to building an inbound organization.

We want to help you.

We want to teach you how to build an inbound organization.

We want to show leaders how to start the process.

We want to explain what an inbound company culture is and how to build it.

We want to show you how to create an inbound organization that can be a competitive advantage in the age of buyer control.

Our Stories

Dan's Inbound Story

I am a business growth enthusiast. I love helping entrepreneurs grow their companies in a way that helps them accomplish their business goals. I advise, invest in, and strategize with owners of varying types and sizes of companies globally. I work with hundreds of companies to help them establish a good culture, define their go-to-market strategy, deliver a quality customer experience, and scale quickly.

My business career started 38 years ago when I was a teenager in the 1970s, selling books door to door (for the SouthWestern Company of Nashville, Tennessee) to work my way through college. The experience taught me the basics of what is now described as a traditional sales process.

The company assigned me a territory in Bellingham, Washington, the first year and Portland, Oregon, the second year. I was given no salary and one week of group sales training. I was dropped off with a few other sales recruits without a place to live, and, without knowing anyone in the territory, within three months I became a top producer for the company.

After I graduated college, I started my career with a regional company that sold personal computers in Boston, Massachusetts. In 1983 my boss quit and accepted a position at a start-up company with a more national scope. He asked me if I wanted to make the jump for a new opportunity, and I agreed to give it a try. This company, Businessland, scaled from $20-plus million and a few locations in 1981 to more than $1.3 billion in less than a decade.

For the first 25 years of my career, I focused on sales, sales management, executive sales management, and general leadership. Running companies during this time was more art than science, more "gut feel" than data; growth rates were lower, and change was much slower.

In those days, the sales process was very seller-centric. Because the salesperson was the central conduit for all information about the product or the service, they were taught to give just enough information as required to get someone to buy.

In 2007, when I first started at HubSpot, I worked in the sales department, selling the HubSpot platform by cold-calling prospects. I called everyone in my physical Rolodex as well as my friends and family. After a few months, new prospects began reaching out to us! So my job morphed into follow-up with inbound leads. This was a huge transition because we went from trying to reach everyone to focusing specifically on leads who expressed an interest in our software by entering their contact information on the HubSpot website. It was a huge improvement in connection efficiency, velocity of the sales process, and quality of life.

In 2007, when I was the original salesperson for HubSpot, people typically had two questions when I connected with them on the phone: (1) What is inbound marketing? and (2) Will it work? I always smiled and explained that the discipline was new, but that it seemed to make sense to me. Also, everyone at HubSpot was an MIT Sloan School graduate and super smart, and I thought it had good potential because I had personal experience (I was an early customer of HubSpot). Even though we only had a few data points, it looked like the new inbound sales process would have a profound impact on revenue generation and customer acquisition.

Inbound marketing effectively eliminated the most time-consuming, low-value activity in the sales process (prospecting) and replaced it with a self-selection process to connect with higher-value clients. This leads to better sales results. Because of the online nature of the transaction, it could be accomplished via the web and over the phone, which greatly reduces the cost of the sales process that traditionally took place in person. Because of the volume of transactions, smart managers could capture valuable data to determine the key points for the specific sales process. This leads to improved efficiency and velocity of the sales process, which leads to a better ROI and lower cost of sales. I started writing, blogging, and speaking about the impact of inbound sales and marketing to thousands of people per year. I quickly realized that the foundation of the process was a philosophy of acting with transparency, focusing on the customer, and providing value before you asked for remuneration. In fact, I authored a blog article titled "Always Be Closing Is Dead: How to Always Be Helping" in 2015 that was very successful in explaining the philosophy and impact.

This new philosophy of leveraging a data-driven engagement process of attracting total strangers and turning them into delighted customers resonated with many people in the audience. Todd was one of those people. After a presentation in California in 2016, he mentioned that he had been working with companies on some of the same types of issues for many years. So, in an effort to share our experiences and help more companies, we decided to commit our observations, thoughts, ideas, and opinions to this book.

Now, 11 years into the inbound revolution, it is easy to answer both questions that people asked me in 2007. Inbound does work, and we can prove it. We know that companies that practice inbound have a clear competitive advantage.

Over the next few years, every company will face a choice. Companies can continue to lean into the traditional way they market, sell, and support, or they can adopt a new philosophy to leverage that competitive advantage.

@dantyre
https://www.linkedin.com/in/dantyre01/
Dantyre1 (Instagram)
dtyre1 (Snapchat)
http://inboundorganization.com/

Todd's Inbound Story

I founded Top Line Results, a consulting firm specializing in helping companies change and grow using inbound marketing and best practice growth strategies. Top Line Results has helped hundreds of clients grow their businesses over the past nine years. We still work with many of our first clients, so we understand how to deliver results over time and how adopting an inbound mindset across the entire organization is critical. We were an early partner of HubSpot, and we cut our inbound teeth with the people at HubSpot who later rose to senior management. We coach, mentor, assist, consult, and deliver marketing and sales results for our clients every day, and we use HubSpot to help them do it.

Not long after we launched our company, we realized there was a need in our target marketplace. Many organizations were experiencing flat or shrinking revenue tied to inefficient demand generation and lead creation. No surprise there: it was 2009, and we were in the middle of the great recession in the United States.

What was surprising were the consistent similarities of all of the companies we were talking to. They all cited the same set of circumstances:

Our salespeople do well when they get in front of qualified prospects; they just need more opportunities.

Our salespeople are not able to get anyone on the phone or to let them in the door "like they used to."

Our lead generation tactics are not working "like they used to."

Our website does not generate much for us, and we are not sure our customers are even using the Internet to look for our products or services.

Our budgets are tight, but we're happy to invest in marketing that works. However, we don't know what to spend money on that will give us a reasonable short- and long-term return.

Our lead- and revenue-generation system is all over the map, wildly inconsistent, and built and driven by individuals rather than process. How can we create one that is repeatable and reliable?

There was an obvious disconnect between how these companies marketed and sold and how their prospects bought.

At the time, we were only delivering consulting services focused on sales force improvements, but then one of our clients asked us to help them with their website. It seems they were getting annoyed when I kept recommending changes to the site. Their webmaster (now there is an obsolete title if there ever was one) would charge $500 to make the most minor of updates. So, they asked me to help them find a better way and build a new website.

The better way we found was the inbound marketing methodology developed by HubSpot.

Before we started Top Line Results, I was part of a turnaround team working at a small manufacturing company in Western Pennsylvania. That company was over 100 years old and was in the third generation of family ownership when they ran out of money and went up for sale. I was hired to lead the marketing and sales efforts and was faced with a very small budget, tough competition, a young and inexperienced sales team, and some lofty revenue generation goals from the investors.

We did not have a budget to spend on driving attention or leads, so we had to find low-cost ways of reaching our target audience. We built a site that started to generate leads, and, more importantly, we used Constant Contact to send marketing emails to our contact list.

The phone started to ring. Very few in our industrial space were creating online content beyond a catalog website, and none that I knew of were using email marketing to attract leads. The emails would come from my account and were signed by me. Our database was not familiar with email marketing campaigns, so I would regularly receive responses thanking me for the helpful information in my emails or asking to discuss a project. They thought I had only sent the email to them!

By the early 2000s I realized targeted content creation, an optimized website, and emails delivered to contacts with an interest in our topics were successful in opening doors and driving leads and sales at a very low cost of customer acquisition.

I was experiencing the power of inbound marketing before I even knew what it was called. Buyer behavior was changing, and this experience was my first inkling that the world of selling I grew up in was no longer the same.

I first learned about HubSpot while looking for solutions to market Top Line Results, when I came across HubSpot's blog posts and the free information they shared about inbound marketing. I set up a free trial and immediately realized the power of being able to quickly and easily update a website, optimize content without having to be a web developer, and having simple and powerful tools to manage all of the online experience.

That first client that asked us to help them build a new website watched the HubSpot demo and immediately saw the benefits (mostly in not having to call the webmaster, wait two weeks for simple changes, and then pay a $500 bill)—and they signed up. The next question they asked was "We don't have anyone in-house to manage this for us, will you do it?" We were now in the marketing services business.

We were barely two steps ahead of the client in terms of using the tools, but Leanne—my amazing wife, best friend, and business partner—quickly took control of the marketing tools and made them sing. Within 90 days the number of website visits had doubled, and leads had gone from zero to 30 by the third month of the project.

For less than the cost of one ad placement, or a fraction of the cost of a trade show, the client was generating more leads than both combined would have generated. They were good leads too, ones that turned into customers. And what was even better was the fact that this engine was now running 24/7/365, generating leads from all over the world, and was connecting them to customers in ways they could not connect using traditional marketing tactics. To this day that company is still a client of ours, and the inbound marketing machine we created is still growing every year and becoming ever more efficient and effective at generating leads.

In 2010 we had six other clients and, being a helpful salesperson, I took this story to all of them. Within 60 days, five of those clients signed up for HubSpot and hired us to manage their inbound marketing. Our transition from a sales consulting company to a revenue growth and inbound marketing consulting and delivery company had begun.

Fast forward eight years. After much success delivering inbound marketing results for our clients and consulting with hundreds of others on how to do inbound marketing and sales, we see the need for the next stage in the process for these companies.

Please go to InboundOrganization.com for free bonus content.

https://www.top-line-results.com/
@toddhockenberry
https://www.linkedin.com/in/toddhockenberry/
http://inboundorganization.com/

Acknowledgments

Anyone who writes a book knows the time and effort required, meaning families are part of the process too.

We want to thank our wives for their patience and support throughout this process.

From Dan: Amy Tyre, thank you for constant personal encouragement, vocabulary help, yoga instruction, and worldly advice.

From Todd: Leanne Hockenberry, thank you for making us the best team I have ever been a part of and for lovingly providing the support I needed to write this book. And thank you for creating the endnotes and compiling the final manuscript.

Our deepest gratitude goes to Rebecca Miller for her editing efforts and for making this book more readable.

Thank you to Abby Hockenberry for her research and comments about the drafts.

Thank you to the amazing team at John Wiley & Sons, especially Shannon Vargo, Kelly Martin, and Jocelyn Kwiat-kowski. As first-time book authors, we asked a lot of questions, and Shannon, Kelly, and Jocelyn were helpful and encouraging the entire way.

Thank you to everyone we interviewed. To a person, each contributed significantly to this book, and we value your insights, appreciate your commitment to inbound, and thank you for helping us:

Adele Revella	Adam Robinson	Eric Baum
Marcus Sheridan	Stormie Andrews	Pete Caputa
Suneera Madhani	Darrell Evans	Bob Ruffolo
Liz Connett	Stacey Ferreira	Natalie Davis

Glenn Williams	Amelia Wilcox	Paul Roetzer
Erik Bjornstad	Francis Pilon	Jack Derby
Mike Thomas	John McTigue	Preston Bowman

Thanks to all of the generous and genuinely helpful people at HubSpot:

Frank Auger	Mark Kilens	Michael Redbord
Katie Burke	Janessa Lantz	Eric Richard
Justin Champion	Rachel Leist	JD Sherman
Brad Coffey	Andrew Mahon	Brian Signorelli
Nathaniel Eberle	David McNeil	Iliyana Stareva
Alison Elworthy	Juliana Nicholson	Corey Wainwright
Michael Ewing	Lorrie Norrington	David Weinhaus
Hannah Fleischman	Meg Prater	Leslie Ye
John Kelleher	Andrew Quinn	

And thank you last, and certainly not least, to the people who started this revolution: Dharmesh Shah and Brian Halligan.

Introduction

Suneera Madhani worked in the merchant service industry and hated everything about it.

She disliked the nickel-and-dime, disdainful attitude her company had toward customers. She didn't like the way the products were delivered. She didn't like the way the company, and every one of their competitors, marketed their services. She didn't like the lack of transparency and honesty about the products, prices, and services. She hated the fact that customers never knew what was going on in the black box that the merchant services company presented. She didn't like the environment she was working in. She didn't like the impact she was having—or not having—on her customers.

She felt that customers deserved better.

She took her ideas for a new way of providing merchant services to her boss. Her ideas were rejected out of hand.

She channeled her frustration, ideas, and innovations into building a merchant services company she could be proud of—and hoped her customers would love it too.

She started Fattmerchant in 2014 with the idea that any business should be able to access merchant services and accept credit cards regardless of their size. She believed that a customer's experience using the service should be simple, powerful, and fun.

She knew she had to have a different approach to building her company, culture, products, strategy, team, and how they went about scaling their business while servicing their customers.

The approach she chose was inbound.

Madhani believed in a subscription model versus the fixed cost approach of the old-school merchant services industry. Because she had seen many customers' frustrations with the poor customer experience inherent in the old model, she believed buyers would be quick to adopt a more customer-centered approach.

"We exist for small- to medium-size business to help them grow; everything else about our growth, our profit, and all of our success flows from that focus,"[1] says Madhani.

She believed the pay-as-you-go subscription model was modern and matched the way people wanted to purchase merchant services.

Liz Connett, marketing manager for Fattmerchant, explains it this way: "We build Fattmerchant's technology around the relationships formed with our customers, who we call members of the Fatt Family, and the feedback they give us. Inbound thinking pervades everything for us from product development to customer service to technology. We built the product based on the specific feedback of our members and the problems they wanted to solve and the relationships we have, and how we make their lives easier, so we end up having a sticky connection with them and their struggles. It all goes back to the inbound idea. It's all about people and relationships."[2]

Fattmerchant's business model is built on the concepts of being easy to use, providing education, and delivering a superior customer experience. They realized that owners and managers of small- and medium-size businesses were no longer willing to pay what they were told to pay by the big banks and old-school payment processors. They wanted a different way.

The value of Fattmerchant's service is putting the customer at the center of the relationship. They base the relationship on radical transparency and opening up the direct cost of the merchant services puzzle. The users of the service wanted to know what they were getting, why they were paying for it, and how the service helped them grow their businesses by giving their customer the payment options they demanded.

Other key service and product attributes that Fattmerchant identified included:

♦ Easy-to-understand tools
♦ Flexible pricing with options
♦ Services matched to their needs
♦ Low barrier to commitment and short-length agreements
♦ Self-service learning and usage

As Connett puts it:

We think that customer experience plays into everything we do for our company. One of our strategic pillars is the best damn experience. We want everyone, throughout their entire journey with Fattmerchant, to have a positive and easy experience. It is something that we are always actively thinking about in our marketing and sales processes even before they become a member. How is that experience going to look to them? Is it easy? Is it simple? Is it clear? Are we talking to them in the tone that they like and appreciate?

Every campaign we run, every strategy we put in place, we build around the customer experience. We ask how can we give our potential new members, our advocates, our part-ners, our employees, or whatever they might end up becom-ing—how can we give them the best experience?

Fattmerchant focuses on a few specific personas and matches their messaging and content to the specific needs of that persona.

For example, Joe's Pizza Shop needs a good experience at the counter for his customers, easy and fast. He also wants to connect to a traditional terminal and have few technical details to worry about. He wants the reporting and accounting to be simple and easy to understand. And he wants to save as much money as possible.

Lawyer Linda has other needs. She wants to simplify transactions for her clients and integrate with the firm's existing accounting systems for detailed reporting and financial analysis. She cares about how the product works and wants to know where costs are coming from but not necessarily use the lowest cost service. She is prepared to pay for more features that provide seamless payment options for her as well as robust integration with their internal systems.

With a huge potential market and many types of personas, Fattmerchant believes detailed persona development is critical because "if you are talking to everyone you are talking to no one," says Madhani.

Personas do not just inform the marketing and sales process at Fattmerchant. Everyone at the company, including legal, finance, operations, service, and engineering, is aware of the target personas and their role in delivering on their mantra of "the best damn [customer] experience."

Fattmerchant views their marketing team as the voice of the customer. Marketing is integrated into every area of the company to make certain the personas are understood and represented in everything they do.

Connett says, "My team sits in on almost all company meetings. We are the voice of the customer."

Connett describes how Fattmerchant uses personas:

> *We always preach how important it is to dig deeper when you think you understand a customer. Everyone has a target audience, but most companies don't necessarily sit down and have a real buyer persona completely fleshed out. We think a detailed persona makes all the difference in being successful. We recommend that people have a clear*

understanding of their buyer: where they go online, what they read when they wake up in the morning, what they watch, where they go for help, where they live. And what they want from their merchant services provider.

Building the buyer personas has been huge for us. But once you have the persona, then you need to make sure that whatever content you're creating is what that buyer is looking for. If your buyer persona is someone who's looking for a very specific kind of content, make sure that's the content you're creating, and that's what you're offering, so you're attracting the right buyers. We think a big benefit of inbound thinking is the ability to get the highest quality leads, as opposed to just the whole fire hose of contacts that you've got to sift through. Truly understanding our buyer personas and making sure that they are driving our decisions is critical.

We are always looking back and asking if we are creating stuff for the optimal buyer, because we think it is easy to be distracted by what we want to write about, or what we think is cool, or what we think is new, or what we think is relevant. But if it's not going to be something our persona is looking for, then it doesn't make sense for us to spend our time talking about it.

Early on Fattmerchant focused on building top-of-the-funnel awareness content to attract prospects to their website and build trust in the subscription idea. Top-of-the funnel refers to content that is used to educate and inform people searching online for solutions and answers to their questions. They also offered valuable resources such as a savings calculator to show prospects how much they were spending using their current merchant services along with opportunities they had to save by switching. Video is another big piece of their content marketing strategy. Videos helped make the complex simple and helped to explain the products and how Fattmerchant customers can use them to help their customers.

"From the moment we started the company we were 100% inbound marketing and sales," says Connett.

> *We were a really small team at the time, and completely bootstrapped. We hadn't gone through any sort of investing yet, or any rounds of funding, so at the time inbound was what made sense for us. Inbound thinking allowed us to reach so many more people than if we were to do traditional outbound marketing. Merchant services is a very traditional industry, so it was very different that we were practicing inbound. Everyone else in this space is very outbound in their approach, including doing a lot of door-to-door cold calling. It's a lot of walking into a business with flyers, sending mailers, things like that. Our inbound strategy let us reach so many more people and have a bigger impact than anything we could do with the number of people we had on our team or the dollar amount that we had at the time.*

> *Everybody from the CEO to the finance team, to product development, to service, every single person in the company is aligned around the idea of using content to educate and help buyers. All content is built based on the buyer journey and persona research discovered by talking to the people that are having issues with old school payment-processing companies.*

Relationships with Fattmerchant customers are built on conversations that uncover ongoing opportunities to solve more of their problems.

"We keep a really open dialogue with our customers, whether it's attending events with them or going to have coffee with someone. Or, if they're on the other side of the country, getting on the phone with them and talking to them. Keeping that open dialogue always top of mind for everyone on our team really drives the success of our inbound effort. Inbound thinking allows us to really understand our target audience and their interests, what they're looking at, what they want to know," says Ms. Connett.

Fattmerchant thinks the process of making their customers successful starts the moment the decision is made to work together. Marketing works alongside the customer success manager (a service manager in a traditional payment processor company) to make sure onboarding is done properly and that the promises made and expectations set during the buying process become a reality.

The customer success manager has a responsibility to follow through until the customer sees results.

Fattmerchant develops automated workflows and tools to map the steps to ensure each persona's success with their specific solution. This process includes calls and one-on-one interactions as well as educational videos, downloadable PDFs, and how-to guides. Fattmerchant finds both increased engagement and higher rates of success when key concepts are delivered using video in place of long text manuals. Videos make onboarding and setup fun and engaging for the customers and results in customers using the services and tools to process transactions successfully.

After onboarding new clients, Fattmerchant continues to reach out proactively to see how customers are doing with the products and if the promises made before the sale are in fact being realized. Fattmerchant monitors tool usage automatically and talks to the user regularly to generate a full picture of the health of the relationship.

Ongoing messaging and communication play a key role in developing deeper and more beneficial relationships. Fattmerchant has typical branding and style guides, but also a messaging guide. Their goal is to simplify technical language and facilitate open communications. Messaging and language are important to Fattmerchant's users since merchant services technology can be confusing and convoluted for busy business owners.

As Connett says:

The better members understand what we are talking about, the better they will be able to implement the solutions. Our goal is to take complicated technology and processes and make them simple—unlike the approach of big banks.

We all want to make sure we speak the member's language and use the terms that our members use. We believe messaging and communication must be consistent and transparent to quickly solve problems for our members. Tone is also critical. We want them to feel that as members we are in this together and that we are always available to help in a friendly and understanding way.

"We believe that our customers are not just a number or a transaction but a member of something special, and that means they should be treated in a special way. By choosing to have a relationship with Fattmerchant, people have access to our technology and services, other members of the Fatt Family, our partners, associations we belongto, and our business partners. We consider the Fatt Family to be a learning group that builds best practices and improves payment processing to improve our members' businesses," says Madhani.

Fattmerchant is an inbound organization.

Chapter 1

Doing Business in the Twenty-First Century

People often think it's other businesses that are affected by competition and technology, but not theirs. Or their customers don't want to change. It is always the other guy.

In 2018 this is a very risky position to maintain.

Not only is buyer change taking place everywhere, but the velocity of change is increasing. All businesses are affected.

Digital disruption rarely fits our linear way of thinking about the world. We make plans assuming a set of conditions that exist today and expect those conditions to be stable over time. We rationalize a set of rules about the way things will unfold. Otherwise, planning is of no value. But change driven by technology, data, connectivity, software, AI, and other advancements are surprisingly additive to each other. Change becomes exponential instead of linear. Moore's Law now applies in other places and describes the acceleration of the changes we feel and see.[1]

Change Happens Gradually, Then Suddenly

In 2018 we are in the "suddenly" phase of exponential change regarding buying and selling.[2] Radical change is obvious in our daily lives when we use our phones to research a purchase; ask Google, Siri, Cortana, or Alexa a question; seek out reviews of products using our phones; and compare prices online.

Inbound strategies aren't only relevant to marketers. Engineers seek out other experts discussing technical questions on social media. Designers seek the newest product packaging options from online e-magazines. A purchasing manager looks for component suppliers on an industry website, a CEO of a small business looks for marketing expertise using LinkedIn, and a salesperson tries to connect with prospects on Twitter or Instagram.

The question is no longer whether buyers are changing, but rather how do business leaders build organizations that serve and succeed given this new buyer behavior.

Over the past 50 years, companies have spent countless hours and billions of dollars to optimize their internal processes. But this internal efficiency no longer drives growth and certainly does not help build customer relationships in this age of abundance.

Peter Drucker once said that "the purpose of a business is to create and keep a customer."

Creating and keeping a customer is different now. For example, in the United States:

97% of consumers now use online media when researching products and services in their local market.[3]

93% of all B2B purchases start with an Internet search.[4]

84% of buyers engage in online information consumption and education.[5]

By a factor of 3 to 1, B2B buyers say that gathering information online on their own is superior to interacting with a sales representative.[6]

59% of B2B buyers explicitly indicate that they do not want to interact with a sales representative as their primary source of research.[7]

74% of sales go to the first company that was helpful.[8]

And this is not only a trend in the United States. According to HubSpot's 2017 *State of Inbound* report, 72% of companies in EMEA and 64% in Asia are employing an inbound marketing strategy in response to similar buyer shifts.

And the statistic that best reflects the changes in buyer behavior is that more than 70% of the average buying process is completed by the buyer alone before a buyer talks to a salesperson.[9] This number is much higher for many B2C purchases.

Some people like to argue over these statistics, and there is room for analysis and interpretation. We cite them here not to provide an absolute value of buyer behavior but as an indicator of the trends that are causing problems for organizations that we will discuss.

What we know for sure is that information proliferation, the Internet, and new communication tools and platforms have drastically changed how organizations create and keep a customer. Does that mean your sales department is irrelevant? No. Does it mean they need to adapt. Yes, it certainly does.

Relationship control, now driven by buyers, demands a new response from every aspect of an organization. Some organizations have responded by adopting inbound marketing tactics, some have adjusted with new sales strategies, and a few are looking at the ongoing customer service experience and creating inbound tools.

These shifts in buyer behavior also mean org chart changes for most organizations. Fundamental buyer behavior changes require different budget priorities and force scorekeeping and analytics changes. Management skills must change. The whole company must now be a part of the customer relationship process, not just marketing and sales.

Change is necessary throughout the *entire* organization to deal with these external challenges.

Doing more with fewer resources, managing a multigenerational workforce, adopting cloud technology, adhering to government regulations, managing costs through outsourcing, utilizing more contract workers, eliminating middle management, and managing distributed teams—these internal changes within organizations impact the experience of prospects and customers outside the organization.

Increased Competition from Everywhere

> *More and more of what we care about in the second machine age are ideas, not things—mind, not matter; bits, not atoms; and interaction, not transactions.*[10]

Digital transformation for many industries leads to prices coming down, meaning many products and services are hurtling toward commodity status. And moving toward commodity status means they may be heading toward irrelevance. Margins get squeezed and start a downward spiral that is hard to stop. It is hard to innovate when you are in survival mode.

So many great products and services are now free. Many software products operate on a freemium model, with the base product available to anyone. Everyone expects a lot of value for free before they even consider a purchase. This thinking is pervasive with consumer products and is moving more and more into traditional B2B transactions. Business buyers want a free trial period, a demo model, or more experience with the actual product to confirm they are making a good decision.

A free trial is not only a requirement for software and apps, it applies to other industries as well. A capital equipment company we work with recently installed a complex food packaging production line inside a food manufacturer's facility for a 30-day test period. Three other equipment manufacturers did the same thing. The trial period was part of the price of competing for the business and was done at the seller's expense.

Product quality is an assumed requirement for consideration, making product differentiation more difficult. If product quality is substandard, product reviews, rating sites, and search trends quickly catch up with the company in a very public and painful way.

Business services are commoditized. Cloud computing, world-class accounting software, financial tools, quality programs, design software, management services, and many other tools have proliferated and are available to most every business.

Traditionally, scarcity yielded high prices and uniqueness built an advantage. The digital and competitive landscape make scarcity and uniqueness ever harder to achieve.

Regardless of the macro trends and how you feel about speed or consolidation, there is one thing we can agree on—digital information has put incumbents at risk for disruption. It is easier today to start a company than ever before. People can start a company for few hundred dollars. Any small upstart can drive traffic and generate leads digitally at a high rate with low cost. A website and great content combined with savvy promotion is enough to open the door to new markets and customers from all over the world.

For the majority of businesses, even up to the Fortune 1000 level, this is the new reality.

Chapter 2

Buyer Expectations Have Changed

It's 2018, and it's time to think about innovation beyond the realm of technology. Today, innovative thinking is crucial to improving the way we buy and sell—all while making it easier for the prospect.

—Marcus Sheridan[1]

"No one uses the Internet to research our products," said the buttoned-up executive.

A partner and I recently conducted a summary review of our inbound consulting work for the senior leadership of the European parent company of our client, their US-based subsidiary selling capital equipment. The executives listened as we described how we used great content, SEO, best-in-practice marketing automation tools, CRM, a site content management system, and site analytics tools to grow a brand-new website generating over 40 leads per month within four months of launch. Before our project, the parent company's website was not generating any leads for the US operation.

Not only is the new US subsidiary's site generating leads for the US operation, but it is also generating leads from prospects around the world because it now ranks ahead of the main corporate site for high-value organic keywords. What the parent company executives didn't realize was how thoroughly their target audience had changed and how that audience now relied heavily on search to gain insight into their capital equipment purchases. Buyers searched to learn about machine technology, the solution most appropriate for an application, new features, how to upgrade machines, what other engineers thought of each manufacturer, how to use these machines to better solve their customers' problems, how to use them to create better products for their customers, and many more pertinent topics.

What the executives did not fully comprehend was the extent that search dominated how buyers gathered information all through the entire buying process. These leaders felt that the product they manufactured was too complicated or technical for engineers, project managers, and buyers to use the Internet to gather information used to make buying decisions. They did not recognize that search had replaced trade shows and face-to-face selling as the dominant research process.

Today's Customer Will Not Be Tomorrow's Customer

There is a market conceit and leadership blind spot we hear about in various forms. It is the mindset that search and the digital revolution isn't impacting a particular market the way it is impacting the rest of the world.

We hear it in statements like these from business leaders about their companies and products:

No one would trust search results to help make these decisions for our products.

Buyers will not decide until they see the product.

No one is talking about us on social media.

Buyers need to talk to a salesperson or engineer to understand the technology.

Information online is all self-serving marketing stuff and no one trusts it.

Our customers know us, so they are going to just call our channel/sales/support people.

Our brand is strong enough so we attract buyers through our reputation.

The challenge of today's organization is to create and keep a customer in light of ever-increasing competition. The whole organization. Not the marketing department. Not the sales department. Everyone in the organization.

The inbound philosophy is not just a marketing and sales idea, but a worldview change that guides the entire organization.

As buying behavior changes, the entire organization from product development to IT, to accounting, to leadership, to sales and marketing, to service must change as well. Many companies recognize the need to change marketing tactics, use content, develop a digital marketing presence, and adapt to the ability of buyers to control the process. Few see it as fundamental to the operation, structure, and strategy of the entire organization.

An organization's relationships and customer experience will increasingly determine the winners and losers in a market. Organizations that best personalize interactions and match the expectations of the customer starting with the buying journey and continuing through the entire lifecycle will win.

Are you adapting to the changes in your marketplace brought about by these disruptions or are you just reacting to them and feel like you are playing catch up all the time?

It is not products but the processes that create products that bring companies long-term success. Good products don't make winners; winners make good products.[2]

In inbound organization terms, it is not just good marketing and sales people, but good customer-focused processes that help companies align with the new buying realities and drive long-term success. The best organizations will develop processes that personalize their interactions with prospects and customers and match their position/reality/stage throughout the entire cycle from beginning to end and then repeat the process with that customer over and over.

Adapting to the new buyer reality requires organizations to rethink their customer engagement process from beginning to end and make the entire organization part of that process. Tinkering around the edges will not work. When fundamental shifts occur, new structures must be built.

An inbound organization is built—or restructured—from the ground up to understand, focus on, solve for, and react to the customer's new demands and expectations.

An inbound organization figures out who their ideal customer is and then relentlessly establishes resources to attract them first, educate them second, start the relationship third, add value at every step in the process, and then ensure their success so they can initiate a series of loops helping the buyer solve more problems.

An inbound organization makes decisions starting with the customer and works backward.

An inbound organization has leadership that knows their industry, their customer personas, spends lots of time assessing various stages of customer needs, values the process of developing a customer, and empowers everyone in the organization to make a good-fit, long-term customer happy by helping them achieve their goals.

For buyers, what matters most is their experience with your company and how well your organization solves problems for them. Business leaders can no longer delegate customer interactions to the marketing, sales, and service teams.

Traditional Industries Are Not Immune to the Challenge

Tube Form Solutions, in Elkhart, Indiana, manufactures and distributes capital equipment for the tube fabrication industry. Recently they held an open house with customers from all over the country. The new laser cutting line was the main attraction, and the sales team was excited to be able to show it off to existing customers.

The president of a large existing customer of Tube Form Solutions walked up to the owner and said, "We've researched a bunch of laser manufacturers online and have narrowed it down to two companies, you and another. We eliminated three others based on features, price, and reputation. Can we talk about a proposal to purchase?"

This existing customer of Tube Form Solutions did not talk to a salesperson prior to narrowing his choices down for this $500,000-plus purchase.

He eliminated other vendors using online searches and other available digital information.

The buyer proactively reached out to Tube Form Solutions when he was ready to finalize the details, specify a machine, negotiate the contract, and take ownership of the laser system.

Was the buying process 70% complete before the buyer reached out to Tube Form Solutions? At least, maybe more.

Luckily for Tube Form Solutions, they had adopted an inbound marketing approach and were making the transition to an inbound organization. This buyer conducted his own research, evaluated potential suppliers, understood available options, and narrowed down the list of possible vendors without ever leaving his office or talking to a salesperson.

This process is reflective of the challenge facing businesses today.

Why the Inbound Organization Philosophy Is the Right Approach

According to Mary Shea, PhD, a principal analyst with Forrester Research, the sales department is no longer the sole provider of information to the buyer. As a result, sales forces in the United States will contract in size by a million positions by 2020.

To drive business growth beyond the economy's rate of growth, you need to innovate around customer experience and use data to produce deeper customer relationships. Product innovation and technology are no longer enough.

These changes necessitate new ways of facilitating better engagement with people, using technology the way buyers want us to use it, and a commitment to being helpful first.

At their core, inbound organizations must build conversations and relationships with their audiences by giving them value before extracting value, which may be years before they make a purchase—helping them when they need and want to be helped.

Marcus Sheridan, author of *They Ask, You Answer* and long-time inbound practitioner and marketing consultant, puts it this way: "I really think inbound should be a way of doing business. To me the core philosophy of inbound is simply bringing so much value to the marketplace that the market can't help but trust you. And because of that trust, ultimately many buyers will give you their business. That's the essence of inbound, they come to you because you're so attractive, so valuable, to the marketplace. But unfortunately, most companies don't see it that way."

Fewer and fewer people read print ads, watch commercials, tolerate spam email, or accept being interrupted. For most companies, your website and social media is where your brand lives. Your brand is defined anywhere customers experience your organization. More than the content you post, it is the customer reviews, comments, shares, and user-generated content—none of which you can control, some of it on third party websites—that defines it. Customers care about the experience more than your marketing materials. It is not what you say your brand is, but what others say their experience with your brand was.

Delighted customers share their stories. They interact with others who may be considering buying from you. Any gap between the experience buyers expect and the one they receive will be publicized online.

The problem for companies is the growing disconnect between the buyer's behavior and their organizational mindset and corporate structure. The clear majority of businesses still allow their organizations to treat their customers in ways they would never want to be treated. Think of all the spam email, unwanted phone calls, poor service practices, annoying voice mail systems that keep buyers from talking to an actual person, wasted junk mail campaigns, buyer-repelling company policies, and the many more types of out-of-date strategies and processes you experience on a daily basis.

You need to establish a new foundation for your organization that reflects the reality of the new buyer. The only way to build competitive advantage is to be inbound so you can do inbound.

Inbound organizations are less affected by increased competition because they rely on the customer experience rather than product features to create competitive advantage. It is harder for competitors to copy this type of innovation—companies must foster it by building trust, over time, through conversations and relationships. How often do you switch from a helpful supplier with whom you have a good relationship and a history of excellent experiences? Periodically you might test the market, but with all of the things pressing you for time, it is unlikely that you would switch from a quality relationship without a very good reason.

Inbound matches the reality you are operating in today. That is why it is the right approach for companies to connect with buyers in the digital age.

Chapter 3

The Building Blocks of an Inbound Organization

An inbound organization creates competitive advantage in the age of buyer control by building relationships with employees, prospects, buyers, and partners and intentionally designs a personalized experience to help them reach their goals.

An inbound organization is guided by a philosophy, a set of core beliefs, and best practices that impact every person in every department to provide value and build trust with customers, partners, and anyone they touch.

An inbound organization leverages a centralized view of the customer to provide a personalized, proactive, and persona-based interaction that enhances the buyer's journey to create an extraordinary experience over the life of the relationship.

The concept of inbound was originally defined in 2007 in relation to the narrow discipline of marketing, recently expanding into sales and service.

Inbound is defined within specific disciplines:

♦ **Inbound marketing**—attracting customers through creating and sharing content that is relevant and helpful, and not interrupting to build trust.

14

- **Inbound sales**—a modern, buyer-centric form of sales where the seller prioritizes the buyer's needs ahead of their own. Inbound salespeople focus on the buyer's pain and context above all else, customizing their sales process and solution, should one exist.
- **Inbound service**—delivering an exceptional customer experience after the point of sale by helping buyers see success in solving their problems.

Inbound impacts everyone in a company including finance, accounting, legal, engineering, human resources, and production. Everyone.

There are also core beliefs that define an inbound organization. These beliefs are:

- Helping others is the right thing to do regardless of your economic self-interest.
- Focus beats bandwidth.
- Treat people like human beings.
- Solve for the customer.
- The full customer experience is your best sustainable competitive advantage.
- Collection and evaluation of data yields the best decisions.

Being an inbound organization means focusing on the goals and aspirations of employees and customers and creating a company, a culture, a product, a service, and an ecosystem that is attractive to those who share your beliefs and are aligned with your purpose and vision of success. These beliefs dictate your culture and guide your team and individual's behavior.

The Disruptive Impact of Inbound
HubSpot cofounder and CEO Brian Halligan is credited with creating *inbound marketing* as a term of art. His ideas, in

conjunction with marketing theories defined by his partner, Dharmesh Shah, and by HubSpot special advisor David Meerman Scott, guided the formation of HubSpot over twelve years ago. A HubSpot marketing director at the time sent David Meerman Scott an email saying, "We just started a company based on your ideas about changing buyer behavior," and the revolution had a name.

> *When HubSpot marketing software debuted in 2007 lots of people thought it was just a piece of software. It soon became apparent that it was much more than a marketing tool. HubSpot and the inbound marketing methodology became a welcome resource for organizations impacted by the sea change in buying behavior. Inbound represented a new way of thinking about how to start conversations, build relationships, and organize business activities. Over time inbound became a philosophy and set of best practices that offered practitioners something of immense value: a competitive advantage. For the first time in our lifetime, inbound marketing gave small- to medium-sized businesses the ability to compete and win against much bigger companies with much larger advertising and marketing budgets. Inbound marketing leveled the buyer attention playing field, because "inbound is about the size of your brain, not the width of your wallet."[1]*

Inbound marketing helped early adopters build tremendous value for their buyers and consequently for themselves by gaining first mover advantage. These inbound marketing pioneers built content and dominated SEO for their target niches and generated the lion's share of attention leading to long-term relationships with buyers. Relationships were based on helping, educating, and advising as opposed to interrupting, annoying, and closing.

Since its inception, inbound has disrupted virtually every vertical and horizontal market for hundreds of thousands of companies in more than 130 countries. This disruption is not just driven by technology but by the companies that use technology to create a superior, remarkable, and memorable customer experience. Inbound has a dramatic impact on every industry associated with outbound or interruptive marketing including advertising, publishing, media, PR, trade associations, and marketing agencies.

Inbound has revolutionized how companies go to market, communicate with prospects, and sell. But it goes beyond just having prospects find you online. Inbound reflects the idea that the customer experience is the key to differentiation in the marketplace. Inbound is about being helpful first and taking the long-term view of the customer relationship.

In this age of buyer control, disruption is not just driven by technology but by the companies that use technology to create a superior, remarkable, and memorable customer experience.

Many startup companies intuitively understand these concepts and build inbound organizations from day one. Look at the major stock indexes and the fastest growing companies in the headlines today. How many of these companies vaulted to success by rethinking the customer experience? Many of the names of hypergrowth companies from the past 20 years did just that: Amazon, Google, Uber, Zappos, Netflix, Spotify, HubSpot.

The average lifespan of companies listed in the S&P 500 index of US companies has decreased from 67 years in the 1920s to just 15 years today.[2]

Why? You know why, because you use these companies for one specific reason: they offer a superior customer experience.

Organizations with years of experience with a product-based strategy, layers of bureaucracy, and outdated policies may find it hard to become inbound, but it can and does happen. We will see examples later in this book of companies new and old, one over 100 years old, moving toward becoming an inbound organization.

"Customer experience is the new marketing."[3] And as a result, organizations must build systems and processes that reflect this new reality.

The problem is that 91% of unhappy customers won't complain—they simply leave,[4] so customer experience is more important than ever before.

We believe that this is the best time to be a business owner, an entrepreneur, a marketer, a salesperson, or a service person—you have the tools to deliver great customer experiences that result in lasting customer relationships.

It has never been easier to start a business. But it has never been harder to scale a business. The winners will be those that are the most helpful to buyers and create great customer experiences.

"We take most of the money that we could have spent on paid advertising and instead put it back into the customer experience. Then we let the customers be our marketing."[5] Customer experience is no accident. It must be designed, engineered, executed, and measured against industry best practices and constantly improved.

The buyer, as well as employees and partners, are now in control in ways that previous generations couldn't even imagine. This is the new business battleground. How to react is the decision that all business owners, directors, senior managers, and advisors must make. Evolving into an inbound organization is one way to solve this problem.

All businesses must make a choice. Follow the same outdated business models of the twentieth century or embrace the way customers buy today.

The place to start is to define your mission.

Chapter 4

Inbound Assessment and the MSPOT

M any organizational leaders and business owners buy into the inbound philosophy. To become an inbound organization, leaders must first commit to being an inbound organization, live the values, set the direction, and translate these ideas into an actual plan that is implemented, managed, and supported by everyone.

A cohesive leadership team that intends to become an inbound organization should follow the steps outlined in the next six chapters.

1. Assess your current capabilities and build your MSPOT (Chapter 4)
2. Start with your mission (Chapter 5)
3. Build a culture that reflects inbound values (Chapter 6)
4. Adopt inbound decision making (Chapter 7)
5. Create an inbound operating system (Chapter 8)
6. Find inbound people (Chapter 9)

Inbound Organization Assessment

Step one is to make a comprehensive assessment of your entire organization. Using the questions and statements in Table 4.1, review how your company and management team conducts

TABLE 4.1 Inbound Organization Assessment

Does your company have a customer-focused mission that employees can rally around?

1	2	3	4	5
We are in business solely to make money.	We have a mission statement printed in our policy manual.	We have created a mission statement that is reflective of our goals.	We have a mission statement that reflects our goals, values, and principles.	We have a relevant, vibrant mission statement that reflects the values of our culture and explains how we help our clients.

Do you have a documented strategy to accomplish your business goals?

1	2	3	4	5
Strategy is overrated.	Our business strategy is to be a good company.	Our business strategy is focused on the effective operation of the company.	We have a well-documented strategy that supports our operating process and guides employee behavior.	We review our strategies annually and implement a plan that reinforces our culture, values, and employee behavior while solving for the customer.

Do you have the right organizational structure to deliver on the plan?

1	2	3	4	5
Kind of.	There is an ad hoc structure of owner, executive, manager, and individual contributor.	We have a hierarchical organizational structure to deliver on the plan.	Our flattened organizational structure serves us today to deliver on our vision and mission.	Our organizational structure allows our people to make decisions closest to the customer, empowering our workforce to fulfill our mission.

Do you spend time cultivating a corporate culture that inspires employees to do their best work?

1	2	3	4	5
We pay our employees, so they should be happy.	Creating a consistent corporate culture has not been easy for us.	We are known for having a quality corporate culture, and we are a good place to work.	Employees feel empowered to do their best work and are active and excited about building on our corporate culture.	We are consistently recognized as one of the best places to work in our location/s and vertical market.

(continued)

21

TABLE 4.1 (*continued*)

Do you communicate decisions effectively to everyone in the organization?

1	2	3	4	5
If managers get around to telling their direct reports, then we are happy.	Leaders make decisions and explain them on a need-to-know basis.	We have staff meetings where we share decisions and expect the managers to explain details to their team.	Our leaders are visible and available to answer any employee questions and we have regular company-wide events to update everyone.	We have formal and informal channels to communicate decisions, including shared digital spaces, company-wide meetings, and team gatherings to share information to make sure everyone is informed.

Do you share essential information throughout your organization as a matter of course?

1	2	3	4	5
We share information on a need-to-know basis.	Critical information is shared with the executive level, and they are responsible for distributing it.	We try to share as much information as we can to our employees.	Essential information is posted and shared in a central repository and feedback is encouraged.	Company information is created and posted in a central repository, reviewed on a regular basis, and feedback and ideas are actively encouraged.

Does the company currently have domain knowledge or experience that provides a true competitive advantage?

1	2	3	4	5
We work in a commodity business with little differentiation.	Our people are our competitive advantage.	We have an easily understood, competitive advantage.	We have an easy-to-understand, easy-to-explain competitive advantage that helps us attract customers.	We have a verifiable, definable, measurable competitive advantage and three years of data to prove it.

Does your business culture align with the recent changes in buyer behavior?

1	2	3	4	5
No, we do business the way we have always done it.	We have made a few changes to react to an online world.	We have a plan to implement changes to our culture that reflect the recent changes in buyer behavior.	Yes, we understand that culture must reflect our intentions to help our customers first.	We have defined an inbound culture as the most tangible way of helping our employees solve our clients' problems.

(continued)

TABLE 4.1 (continued)

Is it hard to identify and recruit good people to work for your company?

1	2	3	4	5
It is a struggle to find good people.	We would like to improve our ability to attract the right type of employee.	We spend a lot of time and effort to recruit good fit employees that understand our mission and values.	It is not hard to find good people because of our reputation in the market.	We have a strong recruiting funnel and onboarding process, and attract the best candidates.

Can you easily collect accurate data to ensure you are tracking against plan?

1	2	3	4	5
We have limited access to data.	We have difficulty getting accurate information because of old data sources and systems.	We have a good foundation of measuring the right information.	We have all the information we need daily to analyze and evaluate our decisions and effectiveness.	Our data capture and analysis is a competitive advantage and allows us to drill into everything we need to make good business decisions in real time.

Do you practice inbound marketing to generate leads and customers?

1	2	3	4	5
We are an outbound marketing organization and use ads and mailings, and buy lists.	We are 75% outbound and starting to practice inbound.	We have adopted the inbound philosophy and are posting content to help educate prospective customers.	We are actively funding more inbound activities as a foundation for new business development.	We have practiced inbound marketing over the last three years to help our prospects and customers and create a competitive advantage.

Does your sales organization practice inbound sales to close more deals?

1	2	3	4	5
What is inbound sales?	We are aware of inbound sales but not sure it fits our industry.	We have started to teach our sales organization about inbound ideas.	Our sales organization understands how to engage, help, and consult, as opposed to qualify and close.	We have trained our sales organization and adopted an inbound sales process to ensure that our customer sales experience is a competitive advantage.

(continued)

TABLE 4.1 (continued)

Do you identify, document, and use a specific ideal buyer persona to focus everyone on a targeted customer?				
1	2	3	4	5
No, we sell to everyone.	We have outlined some demographic data about our customers.	We research demographic information about our best customers and use it to make marketing decisions.	We understand where our product works best and where it does not and understand our ideal buyer persona.	We understand the buyer persona process and track every step in the buyer journey.
Do your back-office business processes align with the changes in buyer behavior?				
1	2	3	4	5
No.	We are aware that back-office processes should align with changes in buyer behavior.	Some back-office departments are aligned with changes in buyer behavior.	Most back office departments are aligned with changes in buyer behavior.	Our back office solves for the customer and knows their role in supporting the customer success journey.
Do you proactively help customers achieve success with your product or service?				
1	2	3	4	5
Not sure what that means.	We only provide service when customers ask for it.	Our customers see success with our products and we have a service team available if they need help.	We proactively help our best customers get more value from our products and services.	We monitor our clients' activity very closely and proactively help all our customers get the most value from our products and services.

26

Do you have a co-marketing or partner network to help you build a community around your ideas?

1	2	3	4	5
We go it alone.	We have a few partners that help us in certain areas.	Yes, we have invested in a partner program to grow our business.	We have made significant investments in a partner program to bring our message to market.	Our partner program is one of the key market differentiators for our clients and incredibly important to our mission and vision.

Column Scores

Final Score

Where do you rank on the inbound organization scale?

16 to 32: There is a lot of work to do to transition to an inbound organization.

33 to 56: Leadership should focus on the core areas needing improvement.

57 to 80: You are on your way to becoming an inbound organization.

business today. This assessment is a quick tool that will help you identify strengths and weaknesses within your organization in relation to inbound principles. It provides a SWOT-like analysis to pinpoint the fundamental building blocks you will need to put in place to evolve into an inbound organization.

For each question, circle the number of the answer that best describes your organization and then total the score at the end to see where you stand.

This assessment guides leaders to ask the right questions about their ability to manage their business with an inbound philosophy. The goal of the assessment is to understand the areas that present the most risk and opportunity during the transition. This assessment should provide insights into your organization's leadership, strategy, culture, operations, and structure to determine how well they align with the inbound philosophy.

Creating an MSPOT

After completing the inbound organization assessment, the next step is to gather your leadership team and begin the process of addressing the gaps and areas for improvement. Leaders need a clear, simple, and concise method of organizing and communicating the ideas discovered in the assessment.

One tool that works well is an MSPOT. This format defines the mission, strategy, plays, omissions, and performance targets in one distinct chart so that leaders can structure, distribute, and communicate this information throughout the organization.

HubSpot developed the MSPOT format as a simple way to take complex organizational, operational, and financial goals and make them accessible to everyone in the organization. There are a variety of different ways to organize this information, but a one-page visual representation works well because it is easy to construct, share, and absorb. A corporate MSPOT builds a common vocabulary, defines priorities, documents key information about the primary components of your company philosophy and values, and ensures that everyone stays on the same page.

The components of an MSPOT are:

M—Mission is a brief statement that defines an organization's vision so that employees, prospects, and customers understand what the company is trying to accomplish. The company mission rarely changes.

S—Strategies outline how the organization is going to deliver on the mission. Strategies define the categories of buyers that the organization is serving and how the company expects to meet their needs. Divisions and departments model this format to create subsets of this information. Strategies are set yearly and adjusted as needed.

P—Plays, or Projects, define the four or five organization-wide initiatives that the company will implement that support the overall company mission and strategy. Each division and team then develop their specific plays to support these corporate plays.

O—Omissions are strategies, plans, and programs that are not priorities for the company in the current year. Focus is frequently an issue for growing companies and listing initiatives the company will avoid in the near term helps people stay centered on the mission. By including omissions in an MSPOT, employees understand which plans have been evaluated and which have been greenlighted.

T—Targets are the specific metrics that will determine how the company is tracking toward the goal. Targets in an MSPOT are color coded (green, yellow, red) to indicate the progress of the initiative, and also include specific numerical goals and results.

MSPOTs consolidate the critical information needed to lead an inbound organization in a clear, easy-to-track format. By

MSPOT

MISSION: We Fix Fuel. Bell Performance exists to provide outstanding products, superior service, and essential education regarding fuels to benefit the world. May the world be better because of Bell.

STRATEGY: We offer commercial grade fuel additives to B2B and B2C buyers by building helpful relationships directly and online.

PLAYS:	TARGETS:	STRETCH:	RESULTS:
Build a Dealer/Reseller network	Expand our Dealer network to include 25 new Dealers/Resellers by the end of 2018	35 new Dealers	
Targeted outreach to B2B companies in the fuel industry	Increase the usage of our Bellicide product in the marketplace by over 300% in 2017	500% increase	
Content marketing strategy to reach TOFU leads	Increase sales for the company by 25% overall in 2018	35% overall increase	
Utilize strategic partners to expand influence	Add 3–5 strategic partners in 2018	6–8 new partners	
OMISSIONS:			
Big box stores and other similar retail channels	Independent sales reps	High-pressure sales techniques to gain customers	
Interruptive advertising			
Any shows, exhibitions, or print media that are focused on B2C users			

FIGURE 4.1 Bell Performance MSPOT.

MSPOT

MISSION: Forge is creating a new contract between employers and employees that offers workplace and schedule flexibility to those working in the service industry.

STRATEGY: Bring local retail, hotel, and restaurant businesses together by helping them share talent in a geographic area that we choose to target.

PLAYS:	TARGETS:	STRETCH:	RESULTS:
Focus on hotel industry in three target cities in Southern CA	10% penetration of hotels in a SIC code or zip code market	20% penetration of hotels in a SIC code of zip code market	
Engage GMS to create local references and define the value of moving off spreadsheets	10 DMs/GMs	15 DMs/GMs	
Showcase Spanish version of the app	100 uses of Spanish version	150 uses of Spanish version	
OMISSIONS:			
Ignore all other geographic locations outside of targets	Stop all enterprise sales pursuits	Delay deployment of nonessential product features	

FIGURE 4.2 JoinForge.com MSPOT.

31

putting the vision, direction, plans, and results in one slide, it becomes easier for everyone to share, absorb, and use.

Figure 4.1 shows an example of an MSPOT from Bell Performance, located in Orlando, Florida. Bell Performance formulates, manufactures, and sells fuel additives to both B2B and B2C customers.

Forge is a startup software company located in San Francisco and offers a software-as-a-service application that automates employee scheduling for part-time and hourly employees in the retail, hotel, and hospitality industries. Figure 4.2 shows their MSPOT.

HubSpot CEO Brian Halligan talks about the importance of the MSPOT: "The MSPOT document is useful for lots of things. For example, we look at this document at our management team meeting and use red/yellow/green to mark the numbers. Any targets that are red or yellow, we spend time and resources trying to get them green in the next couple of meetings. We have all our leaders create their departmental MSPOTs and make sure they fit with the company's."[1]

MSPOTs reduce uncertainty, deliver clarity, and drive alignment for everyone in the organization.

The components of the MSPOT tool are discussed in later chapters. An inbound organization has a strong tie between mission and culture. Culture is the energy and motivating force that drives an inbound organization.

To Do

- ☐ Complete the inbound organization assessment.
- ☐ Review and discuss with your leadership team to identify areas for improvement.
- ☐ Build your MSPOT.

Chapter **5**

Start with Your Mission

In the first chapters of this book, we have made the case that there has been a fundamental change in the way buyers seek solutions to their problems. Inbound organizations think about the implications of these changes and create an appropriate mission to define the company's purpose.

A mission is a one- or two-sentence description of a company's business goals, philosophy, and what the company stands for. A mission defines what that organization is and why it exists. It explains to employees, prospects, and customers what the organization is trying to do.

What Is Your WHY?

Developing a meaningful mission can be challenging. Historically, companies tend to define their mission in nonspecific, internally oriented, and overly simplistic terms that make these statements sound generic. Some leaders focus on short-term problems rather than creating a mission that reflects the long-term direction of the company. Some mission statements are so full of buzzwords and jargon that they become nonsensical. Some companies don't even take the time to create a mission and leave it to employees to make it up as they go along.

Inbound organizations are very clear on the WHY of their business. A WHY could include the reason the business started or the reason it currently exists, or what it hopes to do in the future. In traditional organizations, the WHY often defaults to doing more business or attaining a certain level of profitability, or reflects the personal interests of ownership.

We have heard the owner of a midsize business in the central United States proudly state, "Our mission is to get to $100 million in revenue." That is not an inbound mission.

An inbound mission starts with WHY and works backward. Defining your mission makes it very clear what the company stands for. It helps recruit the right employees who have the proper values, attitudes, and interest in working toward that purpose. It creates a culture where everyone understands the core values of the leadership team and gives meaning to the work. Simon Sinek popularized the notion of finding your WHY. He says, "Every one of us has a WHY, a deep-seated purpose, cause, or belief that inspires you."[1]

In markets characterized by the overabundance of purchasing options, when buyers are faced with dozens of choices for every transaction, a powerful mission carries weight in the decision process. A socially responsible mission could be a significant buying factor. Modern buyers expect that all products meet a standard level of utility. They expect products to work as advertised. Buyers often believe that one product is as good as the next. A modern buyer values a relationship with a company that shares her values, without sacrificing any quality or utility. Buyers increasingly look to buy from companies that match their personal beliefs and that contribute to a mission that lines up with those beliefs. Millennials say they are 60% more likely to buy from socially conscious companies.

An inbound mission recognizes that there is a target market that the organization serves. Within this target market is an ideal company profile (good fit company) and an ideal persona (defined person) who has a specific need. An inbound mission answers an important question for this buyer, explaining what the company does for them. The mission is how your company uses your resources, people, products, and service capabilities to help a certain set of people in a specific target market solve a specific problem.

An inbound organization details its mission around the customer's definition of success.

Does your company mission reflect this new business reality?

According to Frank Auger, CIO of HubSpot, "Most companies have missions, but they are often fluff and propaganda. Inbound companies stand out and thrive because the mission is real and reflects the values of the organization. They publish it, refer to it and use it as a guidepost in everyday work. This is an evolution of the workplace over a generation. Back in the day, we were happy to have a job. Today's job seekers want much more than that. They want a mission and purpose. The challenge is that many companies haven't defined a specific reason for why they exist all the way through to the customer."[2]

Document Your Mission

After you develop the mission, the next step is to document and communicate it to everyone. An inbound mission should include all the attributes just discussed and be reflective of the way you treat your customers. It should be devoid of buzzwords. It should reflect the intrinsic values of the company. Organizations must combine their statements about being socially conscious with clear actions that prove this commitment. Your customers can tell if you are authentic or not.

A good mission should include attributes such as who you intend to help, what issue or problem you seek to improve, and how you will help your customers achieve their goals.

The following are some examples of mission statements that embody the inbound philosophy.

Forge (joinforge.com) is a San Francisco–based startup trying to help part-time employees gain better control and advantage from working multiple jobs.

"Forge is creating a new contract between employers and employees that offers workplace and schedule flexibility to those working in the service industry," says Stacey Ferreira, Forge CEO.

The Forge mission is an excellent example because it is very straightforward. It doesn't talk about a product or internal process, or use words that are misleading or confusing. It focuses on how the company is helping both the businesses and employees that it serves.

Stacey said,

> It was easy for us to pull this together. We started the company because we saw that small retail outlets, hotels, and other local employers had a huge problem finding quality part-time workers. To set their weekly staffing plan, they would post a PDF near the break area so that workers could see their assigned work hours a few weeks in advance and try to plan around that schedule. But the problem was that the schedule changed, so managers had to work the phones—calling workers on short notice to try to get them to work extra shifts if someone called in sick or if there were holes in the schedule. Managers spent all their time trying to get the right staffing the old-fashioned way—on the phone. This was very time consuming and inefficient for everyone involved. Employees were in a tough place too and frustrated. They wanted to work more hours to make more money to feed their families and didn't want to have to wait to get a call or play phone tag. There were a lot of balls in the air. So that meant they usually needed to work many part-time jobs in many locations to make ends meet. If we could give them an automated way to coordinate that process, if we could help part-time employees find hours at other outlets or locations nearby, we thought we would be able to build a company that would serve both constituencies.[3]

The Forge mission is an inbound organization mission.

Amelia Wilcox is founder and CEO of Incorporate Massage. This $2 million services company in Utah provides corporate massage programs for businesses in North America and has a clear company mission.

> *Our mission is to make people happy and improve lives through mobile chair massage.*
>
> *As soon as I heard about the inbound philosophy, it struck a chord deep within me, and I recognized it as truth the moment I heard it. The inbound philosophy aligns completely with my company's value proposition, and is an extension of the way we think. I invested in inbound marketing as a way to grow the business because I was looking for leads and customers, but I quickly realized that the inbound philosophy is more than a set of tactics to connect with prospects.*
>
> *Everyone works overtime here to make sure we provide a good customer experience—that is a given. But the inbound philosophy is about how we think and operate as an organization—it's about how we help everyone; our own team, our clients and their employees, and even the local economies we serve. It's a human mindset. And if that is inbound, then that is what we do.*[4]

Bob Ruffolo, co-founder and CEO of IMPACT Branding, a Diamond-level HubSpot partner and inbound marketing agency, talks about the importance of mission development to his company's growth.

"Our mission is to help people and their organizations succeed by learning and using inbound. We went through a tough period a few years back, and to a large extent, the lack of a real vision led to our struggles.

We worked hard tactically, but our people needed a better reason to excel than just the task in front of them. We gathered our people and wrote out every characteristic we liked in each other and what we loved doing with a passion. This process forced us all to focus on what we are passionate about doing, what had the most impact on our customers, and the future effect we all wanted to have in the world."[5]

A good test of the strength of your mission is to ask yourself if any other company could use the same statement to describe their organization. If another company could use the same language, then it may be too general. If your mission is unique to you, then you are closer to the mark. Another test of mission quality is to ask a few employees to read the mission and see if they recognize it as specific to your organization and reflective of the way you conduct business on a day-to-day basis.

The mission sets the tone for the culture. In HubSpot's case their mission is to "delight SMB and mid-market companies by transforming how they grow." HubSpot's ideal customers are small to medium-sized businesses, anywhere in the world, who are looking to scale and need more leads and customers. HubSpot's customers are delighted when they have access to easy-to-use software that enables good fit customers to find their website.

"The best damn customer experience" is the way Fattmerchant describes their mission. At Fattmerchant, it is more than a slogan. It is a reminder of the company's expectation to everyone in the company.

According to Dharmesh Shah, here is what makes a good mission:

Accurate: This should go without saying, but the statement should describe what you do. It should be a bit aspirational, but you have to "walk the walk."

Simple: It should be easy to understand.

Distinctive: It should be yours. Bonus points if it's non-obvious and memorable.

Short: It should be a sentence and fit in a classic tweet of 140 characters.

Future-resistant: The mission not only should describe you today but should stand the test of time.

Inspiring: It should describe a company of which you are proud and want to be a part.[6]

Inbound organizations start with their WHY and build a mission to define and describe it. Then they communicate it through the organization so that it becomes a foundation for the business.

The mission unites everyone and provides an inspirational statement defining what everyone is working toward. The mission offers buyers a clear understanding of who you are and why they should care about you. Mission or purpose driven companies see higher profit as well.[7]

Inbound organizations start with their authentic mission and work toward achieving it with passion and focus.

To Do

- ☐ Identify your organization's WHY.
- ☐ Define your mission.
- ☐ Extend your mission so that it includes your customer's goals.
- ☐ Document and share your mission.

Chapter 6

Building a Culture That Reflects Inbound Values

Corporate culture refers to an evolving set of values, attitudes, ethics, and beliefs that characterize members of an organization and define its nature. Culture influences all business functions from the first touch, through customer acquisition to customer service, and impacts buyers' expectations and goals. As the connected world evolves, culture has taken on a more important role because a quality culture creates employee loyalty and loyal employees generate more value for customers.

Inbound organizations have learned that spending time, effort, and money to create a remarkable culture makes a huge impact. A healthy company culture makes the company a fun place to work, reduces employee turnover, improves recruiting success, and increases employee productivity. Culture keeps everyone aligned more than rules and procedures. A negative company culture can be expensive, inefficient, and hard to mask from the outside world. To practice inbound with your clients, you need to build an inbound culture. An inbound culture creates an extraordinary employee experience.

Culture stems from the way leaders act, not what they say. A powerful way to let employees know the company culture and values is to practice them on a daily basis. People learn the culture from each other: they react to the reward system that they see; observe other employees getting awards, accolades, promotions, and discipline; and adjust their behavior.

"The reason that we invest in culture—and the reason it's our secret weapon—is because we want to make HubSpot a place where the best people can do their best work!" says J.D. Sherman, HubSpot COO.[1]

Dharmesh Shah talks about culture this way:

> *In a way, the approach we took to building the culture at HubSpot is rooted in the same inbound philosophy that we advocated for doing business. At the core, it's about empathy and treating people with respect. The good news is that there is nothing complicated about this approach—it's quite simple. First, understand what kind of culture your best people want and build that. In most cases, I think businesses will find that their stars want the autonomy to do what they know needs to be done, support, and investment to learn what they need to know, and transparency to understand what's going on in the business. And most importantly, a mission and purpose that they can believe in.[2]*

Strategy gets most of the attention for the simple reason that most leaders are more comfortable with it as a discipline, but as Peter Drucker said, "Culture eats strategy for breakfast."

Employees relate to culture in ways that are different from the way they relate to the company strategy. Employees must be immersed in your culture regardless of their location, work responsibilities, role, or position. Culture affects employees while they are at work and during their own personal time. Culture influences employee motivation more than any other variable. In an age of personalized, connected relationships, a company culture is the way that an employee engages with the organization's mission, vision, and values. Today's workforce works for their team, not a boss. With abundant employment options, why would someone waste time working for a company that doesn't have strong values consistent with their own?

In our research, we have identified seven key attributes that are critical to creating an inbound culture:

1. Trust, Transparency, and Accountability
2. Putting People First
3. Teams and Teamwork
4. Inbound Decision Making
5. Using Good Judgment
6. Creating Your Inbound Operating System and Culture Code
7. Finding Inbound People

We will dig into each of these attributes in detail in the next few chapters.

Trust, Transparency, and Accountability

If you don't have trust, you don't have a relationship. In an organizational context, trust is hard to build and easy to rupture. An inbound organization builds trust at every management level and across all divisions, departments, and locations so that trust becomes a foundation of the way the company functions.

"When there is trust, conflict becomes nothing but the pursuit of truth, an attempt to find the best possible answer. It is not only okay but desirable. Conflict without trust, however, is politics, an attempt to manipulate others in order to win an argument regardless of the truth."[3]

How do you build trust in your organization?

1. Expect it of yourself and the leadership team. Tell the truth. Don't lie. Don't fudge or spin. Be straightforward, especially with subject matter and decisions that

are controversial. Frame discussions in simple terms. Provide both supporting and dissenting thoughts on key arguments. If it is important to you, it will be important to others. Make trust a nonnegotiable part of your company. Demonstrate the proper way to behave and how you want others to behave.

2. Talk about trust in company meetings and one-on-ones and watch how employees react. People may tell you they have high trust, but you see by the way they react if they feel comfortable in the relationship.

3. Be transparent with information to your employees, partners, and your entire ecosystem. Teach employees to value sharing relevant material more than hoarding it; define what happens to information misers who use access to information for their personal advantage.

Transparency builds trust. Transparency is the act of publishing and sharing all company information (unless it is proprietary, personal, or HR related) to everyone in the organization regardless of the importance, nature, or sensitivity of the subject matter. It means sharing financial information, organizational decisions, company results, product road maps, operational plans, management changes, project timelines, and all relevant information with everyone in the company so that every employee views the data and has the opportunity to form their own opinions.

Why do you communicate all of this information? So that people don't have to take time to figure it out on their own. So they understand your position. So they do their jobs better. So they don't need to engage in gossip or office politics to understand what is going on. So they model the behavior of open discussion that leads to building trust with everyone.

Radical transparency means you trust your employees to be smart enough to make up their own minds. You are encouraging people to think through various options, making it safe for dissenting opinions, and surfacing a variety of different solutions that may not have been previously considered.

Once you share information, expect and encourage it to move freely around the organization. Expect it to be discussed, dissected, reviewed, and examined. If employees have questions, don't understand the impact, or don't realize how they can help, leaders must be available to help employees understand what the information means.

How can inbound leaders be more transparent?

1. Start with the basics. Create your mission statement and your MSPOT and review them with your leadership team. Make sure there is a healthy discussion around the implications of everyone seeing this information on a regular basis.

2. Ask each department to construct their team version of the MSPOT. Make sure that they understand the importance of producing the information at the departmental level.

3. Share financial information via "open book" management. Explain the generic categories of an income statement and balance sheet so that employees get familiar with the terms. Then share specific financial results including revenue trends, cost of goods sold, gross profit, profitability, expenses, and pretax income.

4. Explain how company growth works, the difference between sales and cash flow, and how the company results impact teams and individuals.

5. Explain how compensation and promotion, employee reviews, and goals will correspond to the MSPOT framework moving forward.

6. Make sure all new employees see this information at orientation on their first day and explain the sensitivity of this information. Define the process for asking

questions and digging deeper. Explain the rules of what is discussed and clarify what is company confidential.

Transparency builds accountability. If critical information is shared, accountability becomes a more natural part of the culture. Accountability is the willingness of each person to take responsibility for their actions, including their decisions and work results. Inbound organizations trust their employees and require accountability to be successful.

In an inbound organization accountability means that everyone understands the following:

1. I know the goals that I need to reach.
2. I am responsible for meeting those goals.
3. If I can't hit these goals, I should ask for help.

Asking for help is an important component of an inbound organization. Internal collaboration is more conducive to accountability than a competitive environment. High trust means that asking for help is not viewed as a sign of weakness but as a sign of strength. It is a quest for the best answers, the most advanced thinking, and the most developed expertise. In an inbound organization, asking for help is a sign that the person cares enough about the goal to seek all avenues to arrive at the best solution.

Putting People First

People First is about investing in your employees, cultivating a culture of mutual respect, and practicing empathy. Employees that connect and are fulfilled, empowered and ready to act, and aligned and in a trusting environment are better able to deliver the experience buyers expect and to build and foster the relationships that create competitive advantage. As Richard Branson puts it:

*Clients do not come first. Employees come first. If you take care
of your employees, they will take care of the clients. If the person
who works at your company is not appreciated, they are not
going to do things with a smile. By not treating employees well,
companies risk losing customers over bad service.*[4]

Cultivating a People First mindset means recruiting people with
different backgrounds who will take a different approach to
problem solving. Respect means that you understand that
employees have different styles and work habits and that
you value a diversity of ideas and opinions. Empathy means
that you have an understanding of the way people feel.

So which should come first, your employees or your
customers? Both actually, as they are equally important. Leaders
must focus on employees so employees can focus on customers. When leaders build an organization that puts their People
First, those people, in turn, are empowered to put the customer
first in all decisions and interactions. People First works both for
leaders working with employees and employees working with
customers.

Dharmesh Shah has this to say on the key attitude change
required to start building an inbound culture:

*The first and most important step is to shift the organization's
mindset to focus on solving for the customer. Make decisions
based on what's in their interest—because what's in the
customer's interest is in the organization's interest too.
Ensure that everyone knows what you're solving for and
build trust so that when people see things happening that are
not solving for the customer, they have the freedom to speak
up. This transition doesn't happen overnight, but the good
news is that it doesn't have to. As you reorient the business to
align with the customer, the benefits start to show up.*[5]

When we asked Frank Auger, CIO of HubSpot, which is more
important, focusing on your customers, or focusing on your

employees, he said: "Do you love your wife or do you love your mother? You do both."[6]

A key People First ideal is to give your employees a voice in how to run the company and a seat at the decision-making table. Katie Burke is HubSpot's chief people officer, and her title communicates loudly to everyone at HubSpot how important people are. Brian Halligan called Burke "probably HubSpot's most important employee" during his annual address at the INBOUND 2017 conference.

A chief people officer serves as the voice of the employee. This person is a senior-level executive responsible for advocating for all employees globally. They have the responsibility and authority to improve the employee experience by hiring and motivating the best employees available, and then creating an environment in which they can do their best work.

A People First environment leads to healthy employee relationships, which leads to healthy customer relationships.

Teams and Teamwork

The organizational structure that creates the best environment to be inbound is not a hierarchical command and control management structure but a group of fast-acting, cross-departmental, autonomous teams that understand the mission and vision. They create their strategies, plays, goals, and targets and then hold themselves accountable to get work done.

How do you manage these teams? You wind them up and let them go. You ask them to let you know about bottlenecks, and you expect to hear from them if they hit a wall. Some of these teams are within a division; some are cross-functional. Some may be remote; some may be in different offices throughout the world. The common thread is that they share equally in the ability to solve for the customer.

"If you give a team a compelling mission, and the autonomy to attack the mission as they see fit, and the support to accomplish this—magic happens," says Eric Richard, VP of engineering at HubSpot.[7]

Inbound organizations thrive on giving employees control, allowing them to embrace an opportunity and empower individuals to take more responsibility regardless of title or experience. It means there is less emphasis on title and more emphasis on skills. It means executives might be reporting to individual contributors. It means new employees lead. It demonstrates that everyone has a voice and an obligation to contribute.

At HubSpot, there are no offices, no executive row, and any employee can schedule a meeting anytime with anyone else in the organization for any reason. Eliminating barriers to conversations has resulted in open communication; it makes people visibile to others in different roles and departments and ensures that information flows in both directions. This openness helps give people the ability to connect on a personal level.

"Organizations that are set up in a hierarchical fashion make fewer bets based on my experience at traditional companies. When I managed at a Fortune 50 company, the only thing I could do was say no. An inbound company provides autonomy to employees with guard rails and makes it safe to share information rather than hoarding information,"[8] says J. D. Sherman.

Once teams are assembled, sync them up to work together. The alignment happens on several levels:

1. Align the organization's goals with the needs of the customers.
2. Align teams/groups/departments with the goals of the organization.
3. Align people with the team's goals.

Andrew Quinn, HubSpot vice president and executive coach in residence, describes alignment this way: "Everything needs to align around what customers and prospects need to do to buy from you—what do we need to do to get the organization set up to help them and get them to buy?"[9]

At INBOUND 2017 Dharmesh Shah told the story of meeting Elon Musk and asking him for advice on growing and scaling a business.

Musk told Dharmesh that "every person in your company is a vector. Your progress is determined by the sum of all vectors."[10]

A vector is a quantity having magnitude and direction. Each person in your organization is a vector pointing in a certain direction and has a level of magnitude regarding effort, skill, and influence.

Accomplishing your goals is determined by the sum of each person and team being aligned toward the same goals. Having responsibility does not make a person or team effective. They must be pointed in the right direction to be effective and contribute to reaching the organization's goals.

If people and teams are pointed in opposite directions, the net effect is zero regarding your organization's effectiveness in solving for your customers. If the marketing team is running helpful inbound campaigns that attract interested prospects, but the sales department uses old-school closing techniques, then the vectors are not aligned. The net result is an unhappy prospect and a lost opportunity.

More common is the situation where people are "sort of" aligned. If the marketing and sales team align and deliver a seamless inbound experience, but the launch or startup process is poorly planned and clunky, you may make the sale, but the customer is disappointed at the outset of the relationship.

Brad Coffey, HubSpot's chief strategy officer, puts it this way:

More often than not, the greatest source of misalignment happens when people are loyal to their team over the organization. It feels right for people to fight for their team. After all, these are the people that are closest to each other, so personal loyalty matters. Teams that struggle or are not solving for the customer tend to put their team first. People that are solving for themselves first, stand out, and it is pretty rare.[11]

Given the same resources and people, increasing everyone's alignment toward the team's goals will result in improvement of results. Much like focusing light through a lens, alignment results in more power for the team to make an impact on customers.

To Do

☐ Build trust by leading by example.
☐ Practice radical transparency with open book management.
☐ Assign a voice of the employee.
☐ Create small, autonomous teams.
☐ Align teams with the mission, strategies, and goals.

Chapter 7

Inbound Decision Making

Inbound organizations solve problems with an emphasis on enterprise value (EV), which means acting in the best interest of the company as a whole and accepting decisions that help the company mission, even if it makes your job harder. EV means solving for the long-term success of the organization so it delivers value to customers.

What does solving for EV mean in real terms? Let's say you are a direct sales rep working on a target account and you are forecasting a deal close date by the end of the quarter. In the final weeks before signing the contract, the prospect decides that they would like to have a partner do some of the services associated with the installation. As the partner gets involved in the deal, they realize that it is in the prospect's best interest to delay the sale. Solving for EV means that the direct rep works with the partner in the best interest of the customer, which is in the best interest of the company. Even if it takes the salesperson longer to close the deal and she makes less commission, she does it because that decision solves for EV.

Another example would be a product manager that is looking to add functionality to the next generation of an existing product. The new functionality will attract a lot of new customers, who have been delaying their purchase until this new feature is available. But the new feature is immature. If the company deploys the functionality in the next product release, the support organization will receive hundreds of additional calls regarding how to install it, use it, and get the right results. Although the functionality is valuable in its current state, the product manager realizes that deploying it in the next version will place a heavy, expensive burden on the support team that would impact overall customer satisfaction. So solving for EV means delaying the release until the next version because it is in the best interest of the customer and of the company even if it impacts sales in the short term.

Solving for EV requires a balance. Many employees would love to spend more money helping customers with no regard for the health of the organization. Solving for the customer at the expense of the organization may feel good at the time, but those decisions may create terrible margins and decrease EV in the long run (see Figure 7.1).

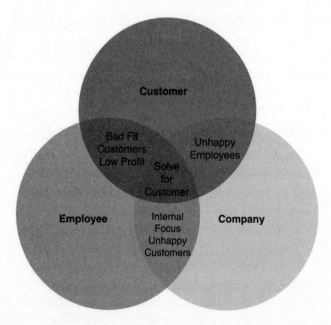

Figure 7.1 Solving for Enterprise Value by Solving for the Customer.

Inbound Decisions

There are three components to every decision: (1) outlining the actual options that you can choose, (2) who is best suited to make the decision, and (3) the timing of the decision. The team members who are closest to the problem should be in the best position to address these three components.

Dharmesh Shah comments on the third component of decision making, when to make the decision:

> *The "optionality tax" is one of the biggest lessons we've learned at HubSpot. In the early stages, we often need to keep our options open, because there's no telling what we're going to run into and the chances are high that we'll head down some dead-end roads and need to backtrack.*
>
> *But, this gets more expensive over time. Too many entrepreneurs (including me) make the mistake of thinking something is a "costless option." Truth be told, there is no such thing. Every option has some cost—it's just that in many cases, they are hidden costs.*
>
> *And, the optionality tax is not limited to just target market selection, it is everywhere.*[1]

It is better to let an idea go unpursued than to keep the option open, draining resources without an actual chance of success.[2]

An important part of decision making is deciding *not* to do something. Identifying what not to do is a central part of creating effective MSPOTs. Omissions are critical to inbound teams because they provide the focus for teams to stay aligned.

Some teams avoid omissions in an attempt to make everyone happy. The result is an uninspired compromise. Uninspired compromise happens when teams take the path of least resistance and refuse to make a real decision. The deciding factor becomes what makes the least number of people unhappy. Decisions should focus on EV and helping customers.

J. D. Sherman describes the outcome of good inbound decisions:

> *There are winners and losers, and people have to be good with that. Managers must help internal groups collaborate and not dictate a specific set of tasks or pathways but let employees own the strategies and plays. If leaders and managers are making all of the decisions, then we know we are not true to our culture, to being inbound, and we work hard to understand why people do not feel empowered to decide and fix it.[3]*

Brian Halligan describes good inbound team decision making this way: "The sign of a good team is that they can have a healthy debate, but once a decision gets made whether they won the debate or not, they need to line up behind it. If you don't have that feature of your team, it is hard to scale."[4]

Sherman discusses inbound decisions:

> *What I spend a lot of time on is making sure that we're living up to this inbound philosophy of empowering the organization and our employees. Much like we do by educating our customers with the inbound philosophy, we want to treat our people the same way. An example would be when an employee screws up there's such an incentive, a natural reaction even, to make rules so that this particular mistake doesn't happen again.*
>
> *We want to gather all the facts, we want to consider all of the alternatives, we want to make a decision, and then we want to move on. At first, this can be hard. People put a lot of time and effort into evaluating and supporting their recommendations, but an inbound culture has a commitment to making difficult decisions, and when the decision is complete the entire company will stand behind that decision.[5]*

Not all decisions have the same impact on the organization.

	No	Difficult to Roll Back?	Yes
Yes	**Big Risk: Easy to Roll Back** *Go if You Understand the Constituency Impact and Can Recover Quickly*	**Big Risk: Hard to Roll Back** *CEO/P&L Owner Must Lead or Delegate but Verify*	
No **Betting the Business?**	**Low Risk: Easy to Roll Back** *Go if It Is the Right Thing for Customers*	**Low Risk: Hard to Roll Back** *Go if Customers Are Prepared; Ensure Key Employee Constituents Are Ready*	

FIGURE 7.2 Norrington Decision-Making Matrix.

Some decisions are more important than others. Lorrie Norrington, lead director for the HubSpot Board of Directors, defines a decision framework for which kind of decisions leaders should focus on. There are four boxes that define all the company decisions (see Figure 7.2). The two axes define importance and permanence of the decision.

All decisions are categorized into one of the boxes in this diagram.

If the decision falls into the two lefthand boxes or lower righthand box, then you should move forward because there is always a way to reverse course if you make the wrong decision.

At the other end of the spectrum, in the upper righthand box, if the decision is a big bet that impacts lots of people, or will be messy to reverse because it has important customer impact or requires changes in systems or processes, you need to vet it out completely with leadership. Work with senior leaders to make sure that you have all of the information, have clarified who owns the decision rights, have thought through all the potential scenarios, and have taken extra time to get it right.

Only the decisions that fall into the bet-your-company boxes, requiring huge resource shifts, require senior executive-level discussions. Push everything else to the teams. Bet-your-company decisions include making an acquisition that could stretch your balance sheet, an investment in an international office, expensive R&D for a new product line, or launching a freemium product needing considerable support.

Use Good Judgment

An inbound workforce doesn't need a policy manual to tell them what to do. A printed policy manual becomes outdated immediately. It is impossible to anticipate every problem or ethical dilemma that your employees will face as they run the business. It is also hard to give reliable guidance on every option for every imaginable problem. Even if you could anticipate every situation, most people wouldn't have the time or inclination to read about it anyway. Employees don't want or need a lot of rules and regulations that define how to behave in every conceivable situation. The very concept of a policy manual is condescending because it signals to your employees that you do not trust them to think through and solve problems themselves.

HubSpot has only one rule that governs all employee behavior—use good judgment. Should a salesperson take a client out for an expensive dinner? Should a software engineer handle a personal issue and come in late? Should an accounts payable clerk take work time to help a colleague in another department during the busy season? Should a product manager post their personal views on social media? The answer to each of those questions? Use good judgment.

Brad Coffey, HubSpot vice president of strategy, puts it this way:

We trust our people to make good judgments, and when they don't we ask ourselves as leaders what did we do wrong, what did we fail to communicate that led to this decision? If you manage this way, you fundamentally get a much more empowered workforce that solves more for the customer than if they were burdened with a heavy set of rules and policies. That is how you end up driving alignment in a culture where people have a lot of autonomy.[6]

What happens when employees don't use good judgment? As human beings, this happens. Bad judgment becomes a teaching moment. An organization that takes the approach of reviewing the available information and evaluating the moral, ethical, legal, operational, and business implications, and then lets the line manager decide, sends a message of trust and accountability to everyone in organization.

After defining inbound decision making the next step is to create an inbound operating system.

To Do

☐ Define enterprise value and explain it to your team.
☐ Organize all decisions into a category.
☐ Watch out for uninspired compromise.
☐ List the decisions you make not to do something in the omissions section of your MSPOT.
☐ Would you be comfortable having "use good judgment" as a guiding belief? Understand why or why not.

Chapter **8**

Create an Inbound Operating System

Inbound organizations need a lean and efficient operating system to function at the highest level, which ensures alignment with the mission and strategies of all groups. An inbound operating system provides tools to support nonhierarchical communication, provides employee feedback, and gives teams the data they need to be successful. An inbound operating system binds everyone together to function as one unit in pursuit of the organization's mission.

An inbound operating system serves as an early warning system for potential problems or bottlenecks. When teams are meeting their goals, leaders don't need to spend much time inspecting their progress. The operating system identifies potential issues, so leaders can get a pulse on how teams are progressing and help keep them in alignment with the organizational mission and strategies.

An inbound operating system is unique to each business, but there are a few consistent components, including open communication tools, employee feedback mechanisms, structured interactions, a culture code, and a regular review of the mission and goals.

J. D. Sherman, COO of HubSpot, describes an inbound operating system this way:

Transparency without context is chaos. I spend most of my time listening and then helping cross-functional teams collaborate. Listening without bias to what people want is what inbound leaders do. Leaders must establish priorities, relentlessly explain the goals, and communicate them to each team and individual. Leaders should work through how teams approach focusing on the overall mission and agreed-upon goals. The leader holds the team accountable, but the team comes up with the plan and executes the work.[1]

Creating Your Culture Code

Inbound organizations define their culture, then document it. A Culture Code is an outline or slide deck that shows the key aspects of your beliefs, values, and aspirations and the type of environment you want to create. The Culture Code helps prospective applicants, employees, partners, vendors, and even customers understand how you view your business and people.

The HubSpot Culture Code
1. We are as maniacal about our metrics as our mission.
2. We obsess over customers, not competitors.
3. We are radically and uncomfortably transparent.
4. We give ourselves the autonomy to be awesome.
5. We are unreasonably selective about our peers.
6. We invest in individual mastery and market value.
7. We defy conventional "wisdom" as it's often unwise.
8. We speak the truth and face the facts.
9. We believe in work + life, not work vs. life.
10. We are a perpetual work in progress.[2]

Documenting your culture will force you to be transparent and to be accountable to live up the promises you make. Documenting the culture signals to everyone that this is a serious subject and worthy of everyone's attention. The Culture

Code makes the details of your culture easy to remember and share and rarely changes.

HubSpot uses a shorthand acronym to communicate their culture:

Humble

Empathetic

Adaptable

Remarkable

Transparent

Documenting culture includes creating a common language for all employees. Using the same terms, such as "solving for the customer," EV, or HEART, provides a common language and is an example of culture providing a framework for connecting.

This simple reminder makes it easy for everyone to frame potential actions and decisions within the guideline of the cultural expectations. As Dharmesh Shah puts it: "Align what you believe with what you say and then do what you say. Grow better."[3]

Andrew Mahon, HubSpot marketing fellow, told us a great story that shows this idea of the HubSpot Culture Code in action. An intern posted a letter on an internal Wiki describing a situation where she was not treated with much empathy. She received many positive replies thanking her for speaking up, and the top leaders at HubSpot listened and responded positively, acknowledging her points and outlining ways they would improve the team's understanding of the situation and how they would handle similar opportunities in the future.

This response sent a very strong message to the entire organization. It showed everyone that leaders were paying attention. It showed that this subject was relevant to more than the HR team. It generated a lot of interest from people who had similar issues or concerns, and it moved the conversations from the back halls to the forefront of company priorities. It epitomized a flat organization structure and how everyone has a responsibility to speak their mind.[4]

Bob Ruffolo of IMPACT talks about their culture code this way:

IMPACT's core values revolve around three key ideas; passion, helpfulness, and dependability. We build our culture by living these values every day.

Everyone that works at IMPACT needs to be a very passionate person about their craft. We only want to surround ourselves with people that strive to be in the elite class of inbound digital marketers, organizational leaders, business growth specialists, design experts, and elite sales professionals. Our people must be completely committed to what we're trying to be as an organization, helping us fulfill our purpose of helping people and organizations, and being a significant contributor to turning our vision into a reality.

To best fulfill our purpose, we can only bring in people that are helpful by nature on to our team and are driven to help clients, members of our audience, and other people of the team. This also extends to helping the community as a whole.

We can count on dependable people. When our people say they're going to do something, we need to rely on the fact that they are going to do it and do it to the best of their abilities. In this business, it's important that we, and the members of our community, can trust the members of our team in any situation.[5]

Natalie Davis, IMPACT Branding director of talent, says, "When we bring new people in to work at IMPACT we tell them they need to get a PhD in IMPACT. We start even during the interview process sharing our mission, culture, and values with candidates, so they know what we expect and what they bring to our culture."[6]

Open Communication Spaces and Tools

J. D. Sherman, COO of HubSpot, talks about communication:

> *We need great communication systems. Transparency is great—but it is wasted if communication isn't great. So, we use a wiki, we have quarterly company meetings, and we have spotlights meetings where one or several senior-level executives are onstage answering questions. It's also a two-way street. It's everyone's responsibility to participate, and other teams need to hear from you. You need to listen to other teams to make sure goals are aligned, and objectives are clear.[7]*

Inbound organizations create open lines of communication. An inbound operating system includes digital tools that facilitate the rapid sharing of information, concerns, questions, and analysis. One proven way to build open lines of communication for a business is a wiki.

A wiki is an internal digital space, a website, where employees collaborate and contribute their ideas and communicate with everyone else in the organization on any topic they choose to share. A wiki is searchable by topic, department, date, subject matter, and even by contributor's name. Everyone in the organization has access to the wiki and contributes by adding new topics with no restriction. Employees can post a new article or reply to a current article. They can ask questions or request additional information. They can alert other members of the team to view that article. Vital information should be posted on the wiki as a matter of course, and departmental managers should also post information on their agendas, project plans, and progress.

A company wiki reinforces an inbound culture and sends a message to the organization that everyone has a voice in important company decisions. Employees are encouraged to share their ideas, thoughts, and opinions. A wiki gives self-service access to conversations from different parts of the company. Over time, it becomes the central repository of data, history, and debate.

Inbound organizations use a wiki to grow a knowledge base around a particular topic by crowdsourcing the content. There is light moderation of a wiki because the users can decide what content is updated, shared, and highlighted. A wiki is a living, breathing manifestation of the state of your culture, your employees, and your organization.

Inbound leaders are active on the wiki and encourage people to post on subjects that are important to them. Active participation in the wiki builds trust, opens the lines of communication, and demonstrates that leaders are interested in employee feedback.

Wikis consist of categories that match the interests and topics of concern to your employees. Examples of wiki categories include:

♦ Facilities
♦ Finance
♦ Engineering
♦ Product
♦ Sales
♦ Marketing
♦ Competitive Intelligence
♦ Collaboration
♦ Partner Program
♦ Business Operations
♦ Recruiting
♦ Operations
♦ International
♦ Information Technology
♦ Culture
♦ Voice of the Customer
♦ Cool Projects

Examples of wiki postings might be:

♦ Q4.17 Product Announcements
♦ Review of October New Product Release

♦ Ideas for Improving Service Response Time
♦ What I Learned at the Google Symposium
♦ Take Your Dog to Work Program

Posting information on the wiki is an important attribute of an inbound culture because it creates legitimacy for ideas generated by anyone in the organization.

A wiki is one way to build an open communication space. Slack and other collaboration tools could also fill this need. It is up to each organization to find the tools that fit their culture because open communication and information sharing is a core requirement of any inbound operating system.

Employee Feedback Mechanisms

Another key communication tool for inbound organizations is the employee net promoter score (eNPS) survey. The net promoter score was originally developed to measure customer loyalty, and inbound organizations use eNPS internally to measure the affinity of employees toward the mission and culture of the company.

eNPS is an effective way to receive an honest assessment of employee attitudes. It is a powerful listening device to understand the general sentiment of the organization and is part of the early warning system when something is not right with employees.

A typical eNPS survey is sent anonymously to each employee each quarter. There are two simple questions:

1. On a scale of 0 to 10, what is the likelihood you'd refer this organization as a place of work to a friend?
2. Why?

Finally, there is an open section to comment or ask questions regarding the company direction, culture, or decisions.

The results of the eNPS each quarter provide everyone unfiltered feedback from employees that choose to answer.

Leaders segment and organize the results by team and group and then publish to everyone in the company. eNPS feedback is a powerful way to reinforce an inbound culture.

eNPS is also an accountability tool for leaders and managers and their behavior. eNPS provides employees a voice, a chance to be heard. It gives employees a positive outlet if they are struggling with a poor leader or manager. If leaders see a manager or team's eNPS score going down, it becomes an opportunity for action. Managers must absorb the information and create a plan to improve the individual issues.

Once a team leader has lost the confidence of their team, it is very difficult to get it back. eNPS is helpful in identifying leaders and managers who are struggling before their team loses confidence. eNPS is also ideal for identifying mismatched managers and teams as well as surfacing deeper employee concerns. A quarterly eNPS survey is a good way to start building trust in your efforts to build an inbound culture.

Employee surveys and the classic suggestion box do not yield the impact and depth of information received from eNPS surveys. These obsolete methods are not automated and take too long to generate feedback. Employees are notorious for ignoring long surveys and are cynical about the impact even if they do complete one.

eNPS works because employees begin to embrace the tool as a way to judge the impact of projects or initiatives they work on. They begin to take pride in a high eNPS score for their project and their team's work.

Regularly Scheduled and Structured Interactions

Company meetings set the tone for effective communication throughout the organization, promote radical transparency, help people stay informed, and are a critical part of the inbound operating system. Gathering everyone both physically and virtually is preferable because being in the same room has a human impact. It's a powerful method of building a shared sense of culture and mission.

Guidelines for running a good company meeting include posting the agenda in advance, starting with the state-of-the-company overview, covering the important initiatives reflective of your MSPOT, giving team leaders the opportunity to present, and spending at least 25% of the time on audience Q&A where everyone has the freedom to submit anonymous questions. Start on time, keep meetings to less than 90 minutes, include remote employees, and share credit and accolades.

While holding company meetings is not a particularly novel idea, the transparent nature of the content and the depth of the information shared in those meetings is what makes them a critical part of an inbound culture.

Senior executive meetings can be run in this way as well; post the agenda in advance for everyone to review, take prolific notes, and post on the wiki. After the meeting, review decisions with team leaders and employees responsible for updating the status of the projects in their MSPOT.

HubSpot holds what they call a HELM meeting once per month with all executive leadership in attendance. In the agenda, each MSPOT has a color code rating for each key corporate initiative, showing the pulse of how the business is performing. The meeting focuses the executive team on the things most critical to the company. If a team is falling behind on a certain MSPOT play, the team is forced to make corrective decisions. All HELM members post their top monthly priorities to the wiki so that the entire organization sees the alignment of their department or group to the overall company mission.

A similar structure applies to departmental and team meetings. A universal characteristic of an inbound culture is a heavy reliance on data and in-depth analysis to inform all decisions and evaluations. A core inbound idea is that you have the ability to measure everything, giving you the opportunity to improve it. Data relevant to strategies and plays becomes a key part of all inbound meetings and interactions.

An example of a highly innovative departmental meeting is the HubSpot science fair. The science fair is a live monthly presentation by members of the product marketing and development team open to the entire company. This meeting allows technical team members to present their work for review, scrutiny, and feedback. Everyone gets to see new product features explained by the teams that developed them. What makes the science fair a great meeting is that it is cross-functional and helps everyone understand future product direction.

A key goal of inbound interactions is a shared review of progress toward the mission and goals. Mentor programs, frequent one-on-ones with executives and employees, product update reviews, internal trade show–type events, and any other opportunity to share the mission, strategies, and plays are important to building and growing an inbound culture.

Inbound organizations create an operating system to ensure the alignment of everyone with mission and strategies. An inbound operating system provides the framework allowing everyone to work together and to function as one unit in the pursuit of the organization's mission.

To Do

☐ Create and document your Culture Code.
☐ Start a wiki or some shared communication space for employees.
☐ Start an ongoing eNPS program.
☐ Incorporate eNPS feedback in evaluation of leaders and managers.
☐ Hold company meetings on a regular basis and share information with radical transparency.

Chapter 9

Find Inbound People

Inbound organizations assign people to support and monitor the culture to make sure it thrives in all locations and throughout all teams. HubSpot set up a culture team to bring the unique attributes of an inbound organization to all international locations as they expanded into seven global offices and almost 2,000 employees.

For HubSpot, scaling culture means focusing on what works. "It is about doing what we say we do, avoiding disruption, documenting our beliefs and culture, and sharing it," says Hannah Fleishman, HubSpot's inbound recruiting manager. She adds:

> *The culture team's mission is to make sure the candidate and employee experiences are remarkable. The culture team focuses on growth opportunities for employees internally, and we don't think about growth as only professional. We want our people to grow as complete individuals too. We want our people to be their best self at work so that they do their best work, and if they leave, they are better for having been here.*[1]

As companies grow, culture changes. Hiring people who naturally embody your core values makes it easy to continue to scale. It is a challenge to retrain experienced workers if they don't naturally embrace the company's values. You don't want to find people who fit the culture; you want to find people who add to it.

Over 70% of Millennials say the company they choose to work for should focus on societal problems, 70% expect to be creative at work, and over two-thirds feel it is the employer's role to make sure they have opportunities for growth and advancement, or they will leave. Most will leave for less money to work for a company that provides these opportunities.[2] Millennials are a mission-driven workforce and desire a strong culture.

In the past, recruiting and job hunting were company-centric. People had limited options for finding job opportunities. Job applicants scoured classified ads in the newspaper, attended job fairs, or leveraged recruiters to find their next position.

Today the vast majority of candidates start their job search by using online search. Candidate-centric searches, enhanced by sites like Glassdoor.com, LinkedIn, and other social media sites, show people what it is like to interview and work for you and your company. These sites include comments from current and former employees and provide vivid details about your company's environment. Companies that put their mission and vision at the core of the recruiting process get the best candidates. Companies that ignore their mission and culture will likely never get the chance to talk to the best candidates.

Smart companies that want to scale use a playbook for inbound recruiting that follows inbound principles. They share their inbound culture as the most important attribute of the job responsibilities. They tout a culture that supports the opportunity for meaningful work, a positive environment, open communications, individual and team growth, and opportunities to develop and advance. Inbound organizations also build a process to attract, engage, and hire top candidates and promote their inbound culture as a prime attraction, sometimes years before someone becomes an active candidate in the recruiting funnel.

A recent study found that 76% of job candidates want to know before they take the job what their day-to-day experience would be like at a company.[3] Job searchers dig deep to learn about your culture.

Inbound recruiting is much like inbound marketing. Inbound recruiting matches the way people research, evaluate, and decide on a new job today the same way people research, evaluate, and buy products. You must research and analyze your ideal candidate and develop a detailed ideal employee persona. The persona outlines the key attributes required for the position. For recruiting purposes, your ideal candidate persona should be the person who has the attitudes, skills, experiences, expertise, and energy required to do the jobs that need to be done to fulfill your mission.

The next step is creating the right content for your company to get found online by your ideal candidate. Dry job descriptions are not noteworthy, interesting, or attractive. Your job descriptions should allow the organization's personality and quirkiness to shine through. Posting a few articles on LinkedIn or tweeting a few stories about your people will not be enough. Inbound organizations must commit to sharing content in a broad way, as HubSpot does on hubspot.com/jobs.

Inbound recruiting attracts talent over the long term. People will pay attention to your company, listen to what you stand for, and then decide they want to work for you to enhance their career. By openly sharing your culture, you cultivate passive candidates and move them into the recruiting funnel, often triggering them to reach out to you.

Getting good candidates is hard for all businesses. Employees with strong cultural attributes are sometimes referred to as *top 2%ers*. Attempting to attract the top 2% means that you are looking for A+ players who have a track record of accomplishment and experience, are able to work together in teams, are status-blind, and get work done. Inbound recruiting is a lot of work. If creating an inbound culture is a priority, recruiting is the single biggest time investment required to build it.

Paul Roetzer told us this story:

> *Not long ago I led in an executive strategy meeting for a multibillion-dollar international company. The room was filled with all of the top marketing people in the organization, from the CMO on down. We presented a one-day workshop on how to evolve the marketing team to inbound. We made the whole argument with data from a few divisions of the company that did adopt inbound with striking results. The data and proof of success struck a chord with the audience.*
>
> *The CMO asked her team what it would take to get the entire marketing team moving in this direction. And then she looked down the table at a boardroom of about 12 or 15 people and asked how many people on the current staff would be a fit for inbound. Mind you, this company had about 300 marketers on the payroll. Everybody just looked around the room at each other and one guy says, "We have maybe one or two I think could handle inbound."*[4]

Your people will determine your success as an inbound organization.

Your number one goal is to find the best people who understand the state of buying today and put them in key positions. Old-school thinking, hierarchical bureaucrats, and fear of change are your enemies.

The only way to become an inbound organization is to be inbound.

So your people must be inbound.

Inbound Recruiting—The Candidate Experience

Hannah Fleischman shares her thoughts on the recruiting process at HubSpot:

The reason I love working at HubSpot is that I truly believe that our founders care about people and putting people first. HubSpot does not think about closing customers but about helping customers. We always put people first and that creates a culture where wanting to see employees grow is the right thing to do.

So, in our recruiting process, we think about solving for the candidate and putting the candidate first in our hiring process. That thinking continues internally when they come on board as well. We put a lot of energy and invest heavily into the employee experience. All of those things relate to how our organization puts people first, not only for the customer but everyone in our ecosystem.[5]

HubSpot sees the recruiting funnel much like a traditional inbound marketing and sales funnel: awareness, then consideration leading to a decision, and then success or delight. The candidate experience is an important precursor to the employee experience.

Fleischman continues:

We design candidate pathways intentionally; they do not just happen. The candidate experience is monitored for effectiveness and adherence to the culture as documented in the HubSpot Culture Code.

HubSpot surveys all face to face interview candidates and asks if they would recommend HubSpot as a place to work on a scale from 1 to 10, and then asks for anecdotal feedback on the interview process. The resulting scores are shared with the interview team, and the process is adjusted or updated using these suggestions. Candidates are also encouraged to leave a Glassdoor review whether they were hired or not. Whether or not a candidate decides to work at HubSpot, we know they will tell their family and friends about the experience. We think that word of mouth is critical to our brand and to our ability to attract the best people to our company.[6]

Top candidates pick the best companies to work for, not the other way around. Much like buyers' access to information, employment candidates expect to research, learn, and understand much more about a potential employer before they even start the interview process.

Mike Ewing, HubSpot customer renewal manager, tells how he attracted HubSpot to him and landed the job he desired.

> *I was working at a family run e-commerce company and ended up out of a job. So, I started researching where I could apply my experience, and I ran across the book* Inbound Marketing. *I became excited about the ideas in the book, and I decided to combine them with what I knew about e-commerce. My next step was to create a blog talking about inbound e-commerce. It was a unique blog at the time; not many people were talking about inbound e-commerce, not even HubSpot.*
>
> *Then I started to connect with people at HubSpot and others in the marketing world and to tweet about inbound e-commerce. I applied for another job at HubSpot and was turned down because I did not have B2B experience. What I didn't know at the time was that two people at HubSpot were tasked with building an inbound e-commerce group. When that group needed to bring in another person they told the recruiter to get the guy writing the blog ecommerceInboundmarketing.com because he was the only one writing about this topic.*
>
> *The recruiter laughs and says we just turned this guy down for another job!*
>
> *The blog was the reason I got found by HubSpot.*[7]

Culture is to recruiting as product is to marketing. Customers are more easily attracted with a great product. Amazing people are more easily attracted with a great culture.[8]

How Do You Find the Right Employees for a People First Culture?

HubSpot is very intentional about their culture and the employee experience. Beginning in the preinterview stage, they send people content explaining the process and expectations. From the first day on the job where every aspect is planned and scheduled, to the last day when lessons are shared and plans made for continued connection to the team, the employee journey is designed to result in an amazing experience for both the employee and the company.

Katie Burke, chief people officer at HubSpot, talks about the candidate experience:

On the candidate experience, we monitor every stage of the candidate journey from candidate Net Promoter Scores (NPS) scores to acceptance rates. Our approach to data within our people operations team is to use full-funnel employee journey data points as leading indicators rather than wait for lagging ones to emerge.

Companies love to use internal data as a form of self-congratulations, ignoring platforms like Glassdoor or InHerSight because they include data points that are hard to hear about your organization. You can ignore external data and employee review sites for as long as you'd like, but you do so at your peril. The scores your candidates and employees leave on review sites are seen by thousands of people each year and have a far greater impact on your acceptance rates and brand than you realize.

It's hard, really hard. You have to really listen, and you have to act on what you hear. You also have to strike a balance between responding and empowering other teams and individual employees to fix challenges themselves. But we view it as the best way to get a pulse on what's going on and to give employees a voice in what's working and what isn't. I think more companies should replace long surveys that don't work with short ones that do. But don't let the most interesting conversations happen in whispers.[9]

Inbound culture is about creating opportunities for people to engage in meaningful dialogue about what matters and what's broken even when—especially when—it's hard to do.

Inbound organizations focus on creating and documenting a culture that is transparent; puts people first; is structured around small, autonomous teams; makes decisions close to the customer; and is focused on a mission that inspires employees and customers.

"Your culture is your brand because whatever a company's culture is internally will ultimately show up in its behaviors and thereby its perception and reputation in the marketplace. You cannot have an exceptionally positive, trustworthy brand without the corresponding culture," states Dharmesh Shah.[10]

To Do

- ☐ Create a persona outline defining who is the ideal inbound recruitment candidate for each position.
- ☐ Develop a candidate journey with detailed mapping of the process.
- ☐ Create content that helps candidates understand the interview process and set proper expectations.
- ☐ Implement a candidate NPS program and use the results to adjust and strengthen your recruiting process.
- ☐ Develop a detailed onboarding plan for new hires.

Chapter 10

Cerasis—Culture Creating a Movement around a Mission

Cerasis is a third-party logistics company providing a web-based logistics management system and integrated transportation services program. They provide tools matching a company looking to ship a package with a freight carrier. Their tools provide customers with the lowest shipping cost in the most efficient way. They give away the transportation management system software, and Cerasis makes their money on the margin of the value-added services they provide—like a stockbroker who provides a free stock-trading application but assesses a charge per trade. Cerasis is a service and software company brokering a transaction between a customer and a provider. They compete with multibillion-dollar multinational corporations like UPS and FedEx. How do they stand out and flourish when they have far fewer resources and are competing against publicly traded behemoths?

They became an inbound organization.

Six years ago, Adam Robinson arrived as director of marketing and immediately saw that the company had a problem: Cerasis worked in reactive mode. They would wait until a customer had a freight claim for damage or loss and then go about trying to mitigate that claim, reducing the cost to the shipper and carrier. He also observed that Cerasis was playing in a market dominated by large, multinational companies, a situation where focusing only on a reactive response put the company at a competitive disadvantage.

Adam started an inbound marketing program focused on being helpful both to the shipper and to their carrier partners from the very first connection. The company began providing advice, support, and content educating shippers about minimizing shipping damage and freight claims for all shipping programs, regardless of which carrier they selected.

Instead of blasting the same outbound messages to all their customers and partners about why companies should be using their shipping service, they started a freight education blog on the company website and created lots of focused content designed to help everyone who used freight shipping services get better information and solve their problems. Cerasis designed content to make shippers aware of the opportunities for cost savings and efficiencies before their products got to the shipping dock and then to ensure the freight got to the right destination on time and undamaged. Cerasis was providing value via this educational content, before extracting value by charging customers, while building awareness for their brand and their freight software and services. Their philosophy was help first, not sell first.

By switching their mindset from optimizing transactions in reaction mode to a philosophy of expecting employees to invest their time and resources into being proactive, customers started to view Cerasis differently. Educating and helping everyone who needed shipping services positioned them as a company that cared about people first, not doing deals as their primary focus, and by extension they became known by more prospects in the industry.

Robinson says:

Changing to an inbound marketing approach by creating helpful content forced us to think about how we could best add value to our customers, carrier partners, and to our *internal team. We learned that our customers don't like pushy salespeople, but they like helpful advisers. They didn't need another software tool or shipping management system; they needed expertise. What they valued was help with their real-time, end-of-line packaging and shipping issues, along with a way to find the best shippers at the specific time on a moment's notice. So, it made sense for our team to move to a proactive mindset that focused on problem avoidance versus a reactive mindset of problem management. The only way we could deliver on the brand promise of educating and helping was if the entire company bought into this philosophy and committed to delivering it.**

The Cerasis leadership team understood the changes in the marketplace (more competition) and buyer's behavior (choosing a vendor who would help them, not only sell to them). Cerasis realized that to create differentiation and competitive advantage they needed to be different than their large competitors and embrace a scalable strategy for providing a unique experience. Being proactive in their approach to their customers not only brought them back to their entrepreneurial roots, but it also reenergized the entire company.

The results of this shift are impressive:

Increase from 45 to 100 employees in five years

100% revenue growth

Website visits increased from 4,000 to 200,000 monthly

1,500 well-qualified leads from the website and blog per year

$3 billion of opportunity per year

60% of Fortune 100 convert on the website as inbound leads

20,000-plus blog subscribers

130,000-plus manufacturing persona blog visits per month

The move to inbound and the commitment to helping people prevent shipping problems rather than fix them gave Cerasis strong intangible reasons why customers preferred to work with them other than price. This became the basis for deep customer relationships built on a better customer experience. Cerasis started to stand out in a commodity industry.

Robinson continues:

> *Product parity ruled our market. Everyone reached a similar level of technology and product features around the same time. What stood out for us (and still does) is our reputation as the thought leader in our space, our value-added relationships with everyone in our ecosystem, and the superior customer experience we deliver. These are now our competitive advantages.**

For Cerasis, their expertise at problem solving, expressed through hundreds of examples of content on their website, formed the backbone of their competitive advantage. They use a "hub and spoke" strategy to share their content internally and externally. They use Cerasis Central to share documents and tools to everyone in the organization. Everyone uses the same CRM system, so everyone has access to the same customer and prospect data. This keeps everyone on the team on the same page with each contact and allows the services team to understand what is going on with the sales team and the support team—they have a 360-degree view of the customer. Externally, the website, blog, and social media allow them to share information with their ecosystem. All communications and messaging use the same customer language of freight claim avoidance and continuous process improvement.

Cerasis realized that a siloed team structure that left customer service people without decision support systems led to an inefficient and ineffective customer process and made it impossible to deliver on the promise of helping and educating.

Service people were defensive and stressed out from having to deal with freight issues alone all day. Moving to a team structure based on cross-functional skills and varied levels and types of expertise helped both internal morale and provided better customer service.

Robinson explains:

> *The inbound, collaborative approach to team building resulted in a better customer experience and a more enjoyable environment for our people. Our people knew they had a team behind them and could focus on making sure everyone won—the customer and us. This structure also led to a bottom-up information flow where the best ideas and solutions to our customer's problems came from the teams that they worked with and shaped the way we offered our products to other companies. The team structure led to even more positive customer interaction, which in turn led to better product development and improvements to our business.**

Cerasis follows a company culture philosophy program called FISH, produced by Charthouse, modeled after the Pike Place Fish Market. FISH is a technique to make happy individuals alert and active in the workplace. John Christensen created this philosophy in 1998 to improve "organizational culture." FISH represents these core values the people at Cerasis commit to living and showing:

Be there—be present for people.

Play and have fun—be creative, be innovative in all you do.

Make someone's day—serve or delight people, choose to be the type of person that serves others.

Choose your attitude—help others internally and externally.

Cerasis holds regular company internal events to emphasize to the team how important these values are and to reinforce them with new team members.

Robinson issues a warning about transitioning to an inbound organization, though: "Inbound is a mindset, it is not something you turn on and off. Inbound can't be about the way you handle your marketing. To be successful, inbound has to be a culture change and something you live throughout the company every day."*

Moving to an inbound approach led Cerasis to measure more customer activity and response times, generate team reports, and create shared metrics and scorecards between departments, even back-office functions like finance and accounting. The goal was to make sure everyone that communicated with a customer followed the same playbook whether they were talking about a shipment or an invoice or the product tools.

Robinson says:

> *We use a common language in communication to customers, whether it's legal talking about contract terms or finance talking about accounts receivable. Our carrier relations department manages our carrier partners who Cerasis works with to match to shipper customers. We are a freight broker, and it is vital we use the same inbound approach with those carrier partners to get the best service for our customers. We even pay the shippers before Cerasis gets paid, so we are building relationships on trust and sharing a commitment to solving the problems of our customers.**

Cerasis believes in building an ecosystem of success that includes anyone they come into contact with, even competitors. Here is Robinson's take on building a network of relationships:

> *You should think of yourself less as a marketer and more as a leader of a community with a bunch of different constituents, noncustomers, and other service providers who are in your space, but not competitive, but have a similar target*

audience. And then, of course, your employees, and then, at last, your customers—all people working together and you at the center, thinking of them as equals and pursuing the idea of always creating value through education and openness.

Cerasis even allows companies with similar offerings to contribute articles to their educational blog as long as the content is valuable to everyone in their audience. They want to be a conduit of value, the place to go for logistics and transportation management information, and are happy to allow similar companies access to their audience if they agree to help and have the same philosophy. Building trust by sharing relevant information is more valuable to them than restricting information because it reinforces that philosophy of helping before selling and putting the customer first.

Cerasis's ultimate goal is to help their entire industry see carrier costs as an investment and not as a cost center and to help manage that way. Everyone wins.

During an internal review process, Robinson asked his team to describe what they do. Here is how one employee described what the company does:

Without taking a long time to write an answer covering the "measurables," I will give a more philosophical take on what the value we bring is. In today's world, regardless of industry, we are all flooded with too much information, whether it is the news (real or fake), emails, direct marketing, texts, other people's opinions, internal company politics, etc. It can be impossible at times to know who to believe, who to trust, what is real, what is important, what isn't important—the list goes on and on. Who can honestly keep up with the information overload at times? Our customers face that struggle both personally and in their daily work environment. It can be very lonely in that respect.

We provide something that in today's world is almost invaluable. Who cares if we are great at auditing, or negotiating, or if we have the best tech? What we offer is access to a larger community, peace of mind, and a calming voice in a cluttered industry/world. With us your world changes; you instantly have a team of people to support you, you have people who are interested in your success. We have a technology that helps you to enable better decision making, and, most importantly, you have experts on your team immediately that don't just understand your business, we understand the market through the eyes of thousands of clients. By working with us, you are plugging into a new collaborative community (Cerasis employees, customers, agents, carrier partners) that you won't have access to if you continue to work in your own bubble. If you work with us, you're not alone. You are joining thousands of others who chose to work with us too. That's pretty awesome, in my opinion.

Cerasis is an inbound organization.

Chapter 11

Inbound Strategies—Change from Selling to Helping People

We live in an age of product parity, material abundance, and fierce competition. Businesses optimize for pricing, have lean operations, and adopt best practices in most functional areas. The opportunity for growth and success will come from marketing innovation by creating amazing customer experiences and developing and delivering inbound strategies.

A strategy is a company's high-level plan for reaching specific business objectives. A strategy is a guide to move to the place you want to be, reach the outcomes you seek, and attain the goals you want to achieve.

Your strategy is the answer to the question "How are we going to succeed?"

The ultimate goal of an inbound organization is to build great customer relationships by delivering an exceptional buying experience. Inbound strategies are based on helping buyers achieve their goals. An inbound strategy is an attitude and mindset that centers on developing the best employee, partner, and buyer experience possible.

An example is HubSpot's strategy to drive innovation around the idea of replacing outbound, interruptive, and annoying marketing by giving businesses a methodology, training, and the software to create competitive advantage and grow.

Companies need to incorporate the changes in buyer behavior into their overall company strategies. Not just your marketing, product, and content strategy but your entire company's strategy—the one that you describe in your mission and MSPOT.

In reality, customers don't care about your strategy documents. They care about how your strategy plays out in their individual customer experience. They only care about how you engage them and help them, and if their individual experience meets their needs. Helping the buyer is your product. If the customers' experiences are extraordinary you have an opportunity to move the relationship to the next level.

An inbound strategy is how you help your customers achieve their goals. Many companies confuse their strategy with their go-to-market activities. The strategy buyers want from your organization is very simple: help them achieve their goals.

Your buyers should determine the tactics you use to implement your strategy. Too often companies get this backward. They chase the shiny new thing. The shiny new thing is the newest social media channel or hot technology that "guarantees" growth in your business. A favorite example of this is "We want a viral video, how do we get one?" Whenever we get that question, we smile and think, "Who doesn't?" The proper way to think about a tactic like video marketing is to ask:

1. Do my customers watch videos?
2. Where do they watch them?
3. What topics do they search to find them?
4. Where in the buyer journey do they consume this content?
5. Which persona does the research to find this content?
6. Who is the best spokesperson to deliver the message in the video?
7. What is the call to action that entices them to engage?

Companies determine strategy. Inbound organizations let customers determine their tactics.

An inbound strategy defines who you will help and how you will help them. This starts before a buyer even knows who you are and continues all the way through the vendor selection, sale, and the life of your product or service. The distinguishing factor in the execution of this strategy is how well you get your entire organization aligned to deliver a superior customer experience. As Dharmesh Shah advises, "Help buyers how they want to be helped, when they want to be helped, where they want to be helped."[1]

Dr. Robert Cialdini, in his book *Influence: The Psychology of Persuasion*, talks about the six principles of persuasion, the first of which is reciprocation:

> *The implication is you have to go first. Give something: give information, give free samples, a free trial, or give a positive experience to people and they will want to give you something in return.*[2]

Backing this powerful principle is data showing that 70% or more people buy from the first company that is helpful.[3]

An inbound strategy focuses on who needs help to solve a particular problem and how to make it easy for them to achieve their goal, thereby helping you achieve your own.

You may have an operational strategy, a positioning strategy, a defender strategy, an opportunity or surfing strategy, a leveraging strategy, a hypergrowth strategy, a brand strategy, a product strategy, a technology strategy, and on and on. But buyer behavior necessitates that you have an overarching inbound strategy layered on top of these to be successful.

Helping first earns you the opportunity to get to the next step with buyers.

When we interview people about the inbound philosophy, mindset, and characteristics of success we hear one common theme: being helpful. Helping is the key to inbound.

An Inbound Strategy Defined

Once you have developed your mission and documented your culture, the next step in building your organizational and team MSPOTs is to develop your inbound strategies.

An inbound strategy embodies the following characteristics:

Honest—sincere, passionate, real, authentic, open, sharing, and understanding that the buyer is in control.

Engagement focused—creating an easy interaction and building a relationship between people. It is empathetic, understanding, interesting, on their terms, in their language, with connection and content when and how they want it.

Personal—focused on a segment of one. Your team knows your ideal buyer persona so well that you know what a great experience means to them and you know how to deliver it.

Matches the buyer journey—starting before the first interaction and lasting for the life of the relationship, affecting all touch points along the way, includes the buyer's journey stages awareness, consideration, decision, and success.

Inbound strategies reflect your commitment to the customer over the features of your products.

Rachel Leist, HubSpot director of marketing new business funnel, puts it this way: "No one at HubSpot is successful if our customers are not successful."[4]

We have all heard that you don't sell a product, you sell what the buyer gets. Or as Theodore Levitt once said, "People don't want to buy a quarter-inch drill, they want a quarter-inch hole."[5] But it is so easy to slide back into talking about creating differentiation based on the superior features using technology or design.

To help buyers, you must understand the problem before you offer the solution. Buyers don't want what you sell, but they do want what they believe they will get, learn, fix, or solve from what you sell. Buyers want the outcome. The challenge in developing inbound strategies is to help buyers understand what they need to change to get to that outcome.

> *Identifying and understanding the job to be done are only the first steps in creating products that customers want—especially ones they will pay premium prices for. It's also essential to create the right set of experiences for the purchase and use of the product and then integrate those experiences into a company's processes.*[6]

A good example is mobile phone data plans in the United States. Are they all the same? Pretty much; they all provide access to texting, mobile apps, and the Internet just about anyplace in the country. Did one network have a superior technology advantage? Maybe for a few months. Did one vendor have a pricing advantage? Maybe a slight advantage. Why would someone change from one network to the other? There is one variable; whether you appreciate the service component and experience of one carrier over the other. If you had a great experience with one vendor at a retail store, over the web, or with your phone, then there is no reason to change. If you had a bad experience, then you are motivated to change. All of the national providers spend millions of dollars on traditional marketing trying to stress a product feature that no one cares about. Can you find one person who has changed a data plan in the last few years based on the power of the network? Look at the recent Sprint commercials where the pitchman says, "Our network is within 1% of the coverage of Verizon." So what's the difference? Where is the technical or service differentiation? It is in the customer experience.

Innovation today is about creating a great customer experience. When technology gaps close very quickly, there are few differentiated product options.

Innovation in customer motivation, preferences, ease of use, helpfulness, personalization, listening skills, and amazing customer experience are rare and hard to duplicate. Understanding your marketplace, ideal buyer persona, the questions customers ask, the issues they need help with, the questions that they don't ask—and wrapping them up and delivering a superior experience—creates true differentiation and long-term customer loyalty.

Instead of touting a machine with one or two advanced features, offer a customer experience where your whole team is so helpful through the entire customer success journey that the customer would never consider going anywhere else.

An inbound strategy is what you do, how you act, and how you react. The actions and reactions show your priorities and demonstrate to customers loud and clear why you are in business and that helping them is your priority.

Be Honest with Yourself and Your Team

Today a large part of your brand is the manifestation of your culture. An inbound strategy may feel like a brand strategy, but it goes deeper because it provides the guiding direction for all employees as they make decisions every day about how to deal with buyers, partners, and each other.

For instance, we rarely see brand strategies influence the finance department and guide their decisions. The same goes for legal, IT, human resources, and production. Inbound strategies reach all divisions, departments, partners, original equipment manufacturers, vendors, customers, and everyone in your ecosystem.

In today's digital age, companies that believe they can be everything to everyone are not being honest with themselves. Being honest is defining your niche and creating demonstrable excellence in it. Being honest is a deeper commitment to addressing fundamental issues facing your employees, partners, and customers and to incorporating or improving internal activities across the organization that deliver a customer an extraordinary buying experience. Honesty means accepting that the buyer is in control and the subsequent implications to your company in the marketplace.

It is easier to bury your head in spreadsheets and financial projections than it is to spend time with customers, especially the ones who may not be happy with your product or service. Being honest means leaders must be customer obsessed and not internally focused. Being honest means being open to buyers and figuring out how to help them.

Think about how you handle customer data and behavior information. Do you use it to help customers achieve success and provide context, or are you using that data to sell, trick, mislead, or confuse them?

Leaders and managers must ask tough questions of their team and customers and then be able to incorporate feedback. These internal conversations must focus on what matters—helping customers—and what obstacles are in the way of getting even better at delivering a great customer experience.

Discussions about strategy must be open, transparent, and public. Everyone in the organization must know what is at stake and have a hand in the results.

Being honest works because it:

- ◆ Attracts the right buyers
- ◆ Builds trust by being transparent
- ◆ Doesn't let you hide behind marketing-speak messaging
- ◆ Focuses you on the things you do best

According to Food Marketing Institute President and CEO Leslie G. Sarasin:

> *Consumers can handle the truth, and the information they do want to know they want delivered in a clear, forthright, trustworthy, and easy-to-find way that conveys some sense of vulnerability and openness. This is a crucial area because I think honest clarity is the currency of trust in the digital age.*[7]

Being honest is a requirement when information freely circulates within your organization. Buyers often share their experience with your organization publicly, so trying to cover up poor customer experience doesn't cut it. Almost everyone has an Internet-connected mobile phone that empowers them as a critic, reviewer, reporter, photographer, videographer, and publisher with a voice.

Developing honest, customer-focused inbound strategies is a requirement to becoming an inbound organization.

To Do

- ☐ Define your inbound strategy based on how you help customers achieve their desired outcomes.
- ☐ Identify obstacles in the way of getting even better at delivering a great customer experience. Define your company strategy in your MSPOT.
- ☐ Document how your inbound strategy impacts a specific niche.

Chapter 12

Inbound Strategies Are Engagement Focused

More and more of what we care about in the second machine age are ideas, not things—mind, not matter; bits, not atoms; and interaction, not transactions.
—Erik Brynjolfsson and Andrew McAfee[1]

In the age of buyer control, organizations have to create opportunities that make it easy for buyers to connect throughout the entire buyer journey. In an inbound context, the term *engagement* means attracting buyers and giving them the opportunity to interact with your content, employees, and products anytime, anywhere. Getting a buyer to choose your product or service over the competition is the goal of engagement, but the key to engagement is being human. Your content, product, and employees must be personal, relevant, and helpful.

The best way to engage buyers is to anticipate what problems they want to solve, diagnose how they research solutions, and help them solve those problems in a fast, comprehensive, and personalized way.

A successful inbound strategy requires defining a responsive customer engagement process with the whole team, including:

- Understanding the buyer's needs
- Engaging the buyer in personal interactions that save time
- Delivering the right information at the right time throughout the buyer's journey
- Offering options for prospects to try before they buy

Connecting Emotionally

When in doubt, connect. That's what fast-growing, important organizations do. Making stuff is great. Making connections is even better.

—Seth Godin[2]

Inbound strategies prioritize this engagement and connection above any product features and emphasize the common values that are shared.

HubSpot CEO Brian Halligan says the following about engagement:

At some point in your business, whether due to scale, timing, or stress, you start going through the motions. Sales reps default to competitive feature selling; marketers ship emails because it's easy, and your entire team is micro-focused on who is doing what and who is getting what instead of why your customers choose to do business with you. Whether you're selling widgets or wagons, software or services, you started your business because you believed there was a why for what you're doing. If that why is not baked into everything you do at every customer touchpoint, you're missing valuable opportunities to build your business and your brand.

People don't buy what you do; they buy why you do it.[3]

Research shows that the best way to create a great customer experience is to connect with buyers on a personal and emotional level by "tapping into their fundamental motivations and fulfilling their deep, often unspoken emotional needs."[4] Examples of these needs include belonging, confidence, uniqueness, being part of something special, security, fulfillment, community, desire for success, and the need for recognition.

Buyers are delighted with small successes, moments of surprise, outstanding service, free stuff, making the buyer's life easier and more enjoyable—all of these help to build trust. The reverse is also true: the smallest inconsistency, moment of disappointment, underwhelming service, or misalignment in the buyer experience triggers an emotional response and often turns buyers away from your product or service for good.

Personalizing the buying experience helps show the buyer that you understand and care about their specific needs. It helps to bring the conversation back to the individual. Everyone wants to feel valued as an individual. A recent study from the University of Texas ascribes our preference for personalized experiences to two main factors: "an innate desire for control and the need to limit information overload in our increasingly hectic lives."[5]

Technology often allows us to substitute digital connections for real human engagement. Inbound organizations humanize the interactions with every person in their ecosystem.

Automating aspects of the buying experience helps companies respond to the buyer and start to anticipate their needs. Buyers want to set their preferences for communication and then forget about it. But we need to be careful about how we automate. It is easy to do automation wrong.

Inbound strategies use automation to facilitate engagement at the buyer's pace. The challenge is to make sure the organization stays connected to the person and continues to present a human touch at all points in the process. Being more human means individualizing your connections with an honest and authentic story. Creating an inbound culture, sharing it with potential buyers, and reflecting those values in each interaction delivers an experience that becomes H2H, human to human.

Inbound is about dropping the facade and bringing the values of the company to life.

It means being more conversational and less rigid. It means listening and being empathetic to the person on the other end of the conversation. "Humans don't buy from companies; humans buy from humans, so solving for humans is every smart company's primary goal."[6]

Are you more or less attracted to companies that tell a story from a specific point of view? How do you feel about companies that show vulnerability and admit when they are wrong? Most people reflect positively on a brand when they experience real human beings associated with that brand. You cannot be a human-focused brand if your culture is not built on the idea of people first. An inbound culture will communicate and deliver messages in a more personal, empathetic, and understanding way.

There are many examples of our emotional connections to successful consumer brands, but the same holds for B2B brands as well.

Delivering the Right Help at the Right Time

Technology continues to create new ways for people to connect and engage in a human way. Mobile phones, email, text, apps, live chat, and Facebook messaging are all examples of modern human-to-human communications. Facebook Messenger alone has 1.3 billion users.[7]

Recent statistics show that 49.4 percent of people would rather reach a business through a messaging app than a phone.[8] And 45.8% would rather contact a business through messaging than email, while 51% of people in the same study said a business needs to be available 24/7.[9]

One of the big reasons behind the consumer shift to messaging applications and live chat is the buyer preference for getting immediate, real-time communication.

Social media also provides organizations with opportunities to deliver inbound strategies. Social media reduces the barriers between a company and their customers. It opens up opportunities to observe, engage, and interact, but it also creates opportunities to embarrass, annoy, and disappoint those same people. Social media doesn't make a business good or bad; it showcases your culture and amplifies it.

Delivering the right help at the right time boils down to listening both with your ears and with your technology tools.

Try Before You Buy

Buyers love it when companies make it easy for them to try before they buy.

The idea behind try before you buy is not a new one. Free samples at the grocery store, test driving a car, and buying a mattress with a 90-day return policy with free shipping and a full refund are staples of a good buyer journey. This concept has led to the buyer expectation that they can try anything, including large B2B purchases, before making a final commitment. Recognizing this change in buyer behavior is a critical component of developing an engaging inbound strategy.

HubSpot describes this as the *code funnel*. The code funnel means providing free software to everyone to provide immediate value. With this model the prospect moves from acquisition to activation and potentially to monetization at their own pace. The prospect becomes a user early in the customer journey and makes a conscious decision of how much time and effort to spend with the product.

The code funnel leapfrogs the education stage and goes directly to the problem-solving stage. It delivers a useful user experience immediately for free. Users can download, install, test, and use the product at no charge and see if they like it. Users are now engaged with a product immediately, without seeing a demo or needing salesperson interaction. It's self-service. It's automated. It's easy.

In today's environment some buyers prefer to skip over the education stage. Some buyers prefer to jump right in and get started immediately. Some buyers prefer more immediate forms of interaction like chat or messaging to get answers to their questions.

The advantages of try-before-you-buy options for the buyer include:

- ◆ Determining if the solution is a fit for their needs
- ◆ Understanding the ease of use of the product
- ◆ Determining the quality of the training and product support
- ◆ Moving at their own pace

The seller also sees significant benefits and opportunities:

- ◆ Accelerates the buying journey
- ◆ Builds a relationship before asking for remuneration
- ◆ Creates a positive experience with the brand
- ◆ Builds user statistics including buyer's favorite features
- ◆ Creates a self-selecting buyer journey
- ◆ Creates strong brand awareness

The idea of try before you buy is not limited to consumer goods, software, or software-as-a-service products. The idea applies to every industry. Buyers choose to purchase from organizations that develop try-before-you-buy options because they have the freedom to research and customize a solution on their own, with the option to ask for help if needed.

When HubSpot asked buyers what makes an exceptional sales experience, 69% said "listen to my needs."[10] In other words, hear me out and understand what I'm trying to achieve. Connect emotionally.

In the same report, 61% said "I want you to share relevant information." Or, I don't need to hear about all the things, only the things that concern me. Be more human and personal, please.

HubSpot also found that 51% said "respond to me in a short amount of time." So, don't leave me hanging. Help me get to an answer quickly. Deliver the right help at the right time.

And 49% said "provide a range of options for me and help me understand all the ways I could tackle the challenge in front of me." Please, don't decide for me what I need. Show me a few options and let me decide. Let me try before I buy.

Inbound strategies build engagement by being helpful, human, and timely, while providing risk-free options.

To Do

☐ Define your responsive customer engagement process with the whole team,

☐ Understand if and how your strategy connects with people emotionally.

☐ Do you have or can you create a code funnel?

☐ Do you leverage chat or messenger apps?

Chapter 13

Inbound Strategies Are Persona Based

Personas are at the core of inbound strategies. An ideal buyer persona is a representation of the person your organization helps the most. Personas are semifictional representations of your ideal customer based on real data and some select educated speculation about customer demographics, behavior patterns, motivations, and goals. Personas include demographic information but put more emphasis on a psychographic profile. Psychographic factors are characteristics relating to someone's activities, interests, and opinions and include common behavior patterns, shared pain points (professional, personal), goals, wishes, dreams, attitudes, and values.

Personas are the basis for inbound strategies because of their emphasis on emotional connection. Most companies sell to at least three or four buyer personas. Personas evolve as habits change. Companies need to focus on their primary personas. Inbound organizations consistently evaluate their personas based on company direction, revenue and gross profit contribution, and impact on enterprise value.

After decades of watching great companies fail, we've concluded that the focus on correlation—and on knowing more and more about customers—is taking firms in the wrong direction. What they need to home in on is the progress that the customer is trying to make in each circumstance—what the customer hopes to accomplish. This is what we've come to call the job to be done.[1]

A persona embodies a person, not a large, amorphous, demographic-driven market segment. Initial persona assumptions are supported by user data that confirms behavior and creates a complete view of the customer.

Marcus Sheridan, the Sales Lion and author of the book *They Ask, You Answer*, says this about personas:

> *Helping is the essence of the "they ask, you answer" idea. We don't base our decisions on competitors. We don't base our decisions on bad fits that aren't ideal customers or clients anyway. We base our decisions on prospects that are a good fit for our business. If that is whom we're focused on, then it gives us the ability to communicate however we want and be totally honest and be totally real. We don't have to fluff it; we don't have to do any of that stuff. We can be straightforward with the information and give it to people directly. That wins us trust, and ultimately trust is what drives revenue.*[2]

An inbound organization helps everyone in the precontact stage. Understanding your ideal buyer persona helps you define your targets, craft your messages, identify product/market fit, and define an effective buyer journey. It helps if you can determine the persona's goals, challenges, influences, emotions, and values.

Focusing on a persona helps you avoid the mistake of selling to the wrong buyer. Tracking personas helps you understand the most profitable buyers. An inbound organization obsesses over personas because it allows them to understand their buyer at an emotional level.

Jeff Bezos says, "Listen to the customer and invent for the customer." In a well-known story, Bezos leaves an empty chair in every meeting that represents the customer or, as he says, "the most important person in the room."[3]

While you may not leave a real chair open at the conference table, your cultural mindset should be focused on the ideal buyer persona and on how to treat them during the buyer journey.

Buying Insight

Adele Revella, CEO of the Buyer Persona Institute and author of *Buyer Personas: How to Gain Insight into Your Customer's Expectations, Align Your Marketing Strategies, and Win More Business*, describes buyer personas this way:

> *A persona, if built correctly, goes beyond what I call a persona profile and the buyer's journey and includes buying insight. It includes the buyer's voice speaking directly to how, when, and why they make the investment that the company wants buyers to make. The persona tells the company what triggers an investment, what outcomes the buyer expects from that investment, and what their objections are to choosing a company as their investment partner.*
>
> *If the persona description includes all the questions the buyers ask about the solution and the company as they go through their journey, then it's really the foundation of the company aligning everything it does with what the market wants. The persona grounds the company in the market's reality, and this is entirely missing from most companies right now.[4]*

There are many ways to build a persona, but they should all contain the key information outlined by the 5 Rings of Buying Insight described by Revella:

1. **Priority Initiative** is the most compelling reason buyers invest in a similar solution to yours.

2. **Success Factors** are the results your persona expects from a purchase like yours.
3. **Perceived Barriers** describe the things that prevent a buyer from moving ahead with a solution like yours.
4. **Buyer's Journey** is the story of the steps buyers take as they evaluate and choose the product, service, or company and who is involved in the decision.
5. **Decision Criteria** are the attributes of your offering that are evaluated as buyers compare alternatives.

How do you start the persona discovery process? The path to developing personas is to interview customers and prospects and develop qualitative insights into the buyer's thinking. The key is: "Go to the source. Get the story in their own words."[2] This direct approach helps you avoid the classic mistake of making assumptions and letting your biases lead you astray. Let the buyers tell you what they want, how they buy, and other key buyer journey information.

How do you conduct these types of persona investigation calls? This type of call is not scripted. If you write down questions in advance, you may miss the most important part of the story. Start by taking the buyer back to the beginning of their journey with an open-ended question like "Let's go back to when you decided to start looking for [the type of solution here]: what triggered the decision to start looking?" Then ask buyers to talk about what they did next to research their options. Keep asking follow-up questions to get buyers to "say more about that" and go deeper to get to their buying motivations and decision-making preferences. If you accept the first answer, you may miss critical insights.

Around 10 to 15 interviews will uncover the insights you need. Leaders should participate in these calls so they hear the answers with the authentic tone, texture, and emphasis of the buyer. Do not let your sales team do these calls because they have a tendency to turn them into sales calls. It is even better to use an outside consultant to do the interviews to bring an unbiased perspective and identify blind spots that you've missed. Leaders should at least read the full interview transcripts and see for themselves the insights in the customer's own words.

The key to persona interviews is to listen closely and discern the nuances of the how, when, and why of buyer decision making. You will hear details of the customer's mindset that you have never heard or considered before. These become the core insights as you develop your inbound strategies.

Other persona development steps include:

- ♦ Analyzing your existing customers' revenue, gross profit, cost of customer acquisition, and lifetime value
- ♦ Determining which type of customers stay with you the longest, purchase repeatedly, and why
- ♦ Learning which customers are highly profitable, break even, or unprofitable and why
- ♦ Interviewing sales and asking them which leads are the best fit and what the essential characteristics are that they look for when qualifying
- ♦ Review trends with marketing to see how people engage with your website, email, and social media
- ♦ Talk to customers that have left for a competitor and prospects that haven't bought yet—because they will highlight the gaps in your customer experience and what your competition does better

The result of the persona discovery process is a personalized representation of your ideal customer based on your research and data analysis. A persona is not just a description of job duties of the person you want to sell to. This persona becomes your guiding focus as you design the customer experience and begin to engage prospects through the stages of the buyer journey (see Figure 13.1).

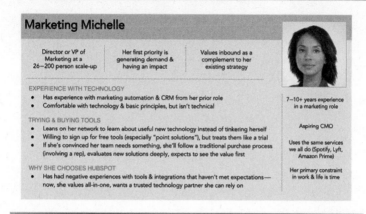

FIGURE 13.1 An Example of a HubSpot Persona Representation.
Source: Courtesy of Hubspot.

Developing an ideal persona is a core attribute of an inbound strategy. The persona discovery process gives your team a strong guideline to develop plays and action plans for your MSPOT to implement the strategy.

As Adele Revella told us:

The goal for buyer personas is to understand how we can be more effective in persuading buyers to do business with us with buying experience being a key differentiator for our company. In other words, so many of our clients are in mature markets where frankly there's at least a half a dozen other companies that can solve the problem pretty well from the buyer's perspective. Let's have the buyer's ability to trust us and get their questions answered be the differentiator in terms of our ability to win that business.

If that's the purpose of buyer personas, and I say it is, then let's, by all means, drop this idea that we need to segment buyers based on their job titles, their industry, their company size, or any other completely obvious demographic criteria and let's instead find out what's different about what buyers want, what matters to buyers as they go through that assessment. Let's get clear, very, very clear on what buyers care about and what would be helpful to the buyer and let's only build a second buyer persona when something different would be helpful to them.[5]

Personas should be updated constantly. Make sure the work of persona development is visible and relevant to ongoing daily work. Document persona insights and educate everyone in your organization about who the persona is and how each employee has a role in helping that persona achieve their goals.

People make decisions for their businesses in many ways— some are go-it-alone types, others develop consensus, and some are a mix of both. Building personas is about finding the critical areas that affect the decision to buy, how the people making buying decisions use information, and how to manage the internal change process.

A persona is the embodiment of the buyer you exist to serve.

How Target Markets Are Different than Demographics

Traditional marketing defines market segments by SIC or NAICS codes and includes distinguishing business character-istics like the number of employees or location, target business roles like purchasing or engineering, and demographics like age, location, and educational attainment.

Modern buyers do not fit into tidy categories. Look around your neighborhood. Traditional market segmentation would say that the entire neighborhood is one market demographic based on location, income, house size, school district, the number of cars in your garage, etc. But are you and your neighbors that similar? In most cases you don't have the same needs, wants, buying habits, likes, motivations, and dislikes. You don't work the same hours, root for the same teams, play the same music, watch the same shows, or care about the same things. There are some commonalities, but the differences are what matter. The differences include the problems that you are concerned about, the goals you want to achieve, and the outcomes that you desire.

The same ideas hold true in your business, whether B2B, B2C, B2A (business to appliance) or B2W (business to whatever).

The more effectively you target your ideal buyer persona and their problems and goals, the more successful you are likely to be. The more specific your niche, the easier it will be to talk directly to the people who make up that niche. You can target tool and die companies in the Southwest. Or you can narrow it down to tool and die companies in greater Phoenix with at least 10 employees, $3 million-plus in annual revenue, who are looking to grow their business at least 30% in the next 18 months.

Entrepreneurs are tempted to say: we should sell to a large market. But this is an impulse based on fear, of missing a sale or being too narrow. The fear is that focusing your efforts means slower growth and less market share and being broadly based means a bigger, more lucrative market. The reality is the exact opposite. Trying to get a little bit of a big pie usually means getting none of it. About segmentation, Adele Revella says:

> *What we care about as marketers is, as buyers consider and evaluate products and services like ours, what resonates with them? What would be helpful to them? What is useful? That's how you want to segment your business strategies. Segmentation comes after we get buying insights, not before.*[6]

Do modern buyers want a generalist or do they want the absolute world's best at solving the specific problem they have in front of them, by an industry expert, who focuses on their exact niche? Think of it this way: If you have 500 prospects, do you consider them all the same or do you narrow them down to the best 10% that you help the most, increasing your chances of a sale? When you go to an event or trade show (yes, these still exist and are great opportunities for many companies) do you try to help everyone? Yes. Do you also place more time, effort, attention, and focus on the best-fit prospects that you meet and give them extra attention? Of course.

Employing an inbound strategy means sharing information that potentially will help everyone, but most of the efforts are focused on helping a very niche market and the ideal buyer personas who raise their hands and say, "I want more help."

You can't convert everyone, but you can try to help everyone in your ecosystem.

Todd's accountant focuses on small family-owned, privately held, individual businesses in Florida. Todd describes his view of the accountant's ideal buyer persona:

> *He focuses on my personal needs, concerns, questions, and goals. He knows the laws and rules as they pertain to our business. He knows accounting, knows how to legally maximize deductions for our type of business. He knows how to keep us out of an audit and at the same time keeps us current on taxes and investments. He knows my business. He is not an accountant for a bank or a large company. He is an expert that empathetically helps me understand the options and issues regarding finance and accounting for a business like mine, and makes sure I take the actions necessary to be financially safe and secure while achieving my goals.*

Dan tells a related story about a HubSpot partner:

> *A business owner in Helsinki told me, "I work with companies that have turnover of at least 10 million euros, at least a six-month sales process, have five people in their sales organization, a partner channel, and are digitally*

immature." When he gets on the phone with the owner of a business that fits this description, it is game over; he wins the business 90% of the time.

Todd tells this story:

I was working to help turn around a small manufacturing company, and we brought the principal owners in to see the latest piece of capital equipment the team built. We were proud of it and wanted to show the new ownership team what we could do.

One of the owners looked at it and said, "Nice machine, are there a hundred people that can use it? If not, it is a piece of art." He was right. We focused on one specific customer challenge and did not consider if this was a custom product or if even one other person could use it. Had we focused on the persona we would have seen this right away. Lacking the clarity of who we were building equipment for led us in the wrong direction.

In this age of specialization, niche beats broad every time. Persona development is about staying focused. It makes it easier for you and easier for your prospects, so no one is wasting time in bad fit relationships or with misaligned solutions.

The ideal buyer persona is the focus of all marketing and sales plans. By using a developed persona, your marketing and sales efforts stay targeted, and your plans stay focused. Starting from the customer and working backward is more effective than starting with an internal goal and working outward.

An ideal persona is a fundamental tool for inbound organizations. Personas apply to your buyers, employees, and partners. The process we described for buyers applies equally to employees you want to attract and to partners you want to engage. Developing specific personas gives you the insight you need to personalize your organization's interactions, which is exactly what everyone connected to your organization wants.

To Do

☐ Define, conduct, and analyze persona discovery process interviews.
☐ Document the insights in a persona profile.
☐ Make the persona profile visible and share it with everyone.
☐ Use the persona insights to test decisions for enterprise value (EV) and customer focus.
☐ Regularly refine your employee, partner, and ideal buyer personas.

Chapter 14

Politics, Personas, and Inbound

Todd learned the value of focusing on a persona and how important it is to inbound success during a unique experience. In 2006 he ran for state representative in Beaver, Pennsylvania. In this chapter, Todd tells the story of the campaign.

We lived in an area controlled by one political party for as long as anyone could remember and, as in all power situations without accountability, the party had descended into corruption. One day around Christmas, I was reading another account of one of the latest insults to the electorate by the ruling party, when I put down the paper and said to my wife, "I can beat that guy."

Believe me, I knew it was a long shot, but it was worth a try.

So, we filed the petitions with the requisite signatures, and I set out on my first campaign. With no campaign money and limited time (I was still employed full-time and needed to keep my job), we had to figure out how to reach out to approximately 20,000 people. Then we had to convince them to vote for me, an average citizen with no name recognition, no formal political organization, no volunteer organization, and no funding.

Against these odds, we developed a very simple and powerful plan. We gambled the success of our entire campaign by focusing on a very specific niche. We did the research and decided to engage only with voters who cared enough to vote in an off-year election, which represented our targeted persona and key to success.

During our research, we learned that voter information is quite extensive and available via public records. We had access to data regarding which people show up and vote each year, historical precinct voter patterns, and, in some cases, individual advocacy for certain issues known to their state party of choice.

As we reviewed the data, a powerful theme emerged. Our best path to success boiled down to targeting a very specific persona. By *only* talking to the people who voted in off-year, nonpresidential elections, and who resided in precincts that had a 35% or better record of voting for the long out-of-power party, we were able to maximize our impact to provide the best path to victory.

We excluded voters if they only voted in the presidential years and we only talked to prospects if they were a voter in over 50% of all possible elections for several reasons:

- ◆ They were more accepting of our message.
- ◆ They were more politically active and therefore more interested in the details.
- ◆ We had limited time and resources.

Note: Does this sound familiar in a business context? Isn't this the same challenge that all businesses face as they scale?

We did not differentiate the persona based on party affiliation because our data indicated that it was an irrelevant measure; the key metric was whether the registered voter voted over 50% of the time. This focus ensured that our message was noticed by those looking for it, who would be most receptive to it.

The "solution" that solved this persona's problem was a new face untainted by the current political machine. It was that simple. For many people in my district, it boiled down to the fact that they were sick and tired of the same old party hacks and wanted a change.

Which was perfect, because our message was all about change. I had to show up and be a credible candidate. In an inbound context, that means we had to create awareness and explain our value in the Consideration phase (see Chapter 15). Being a legitimate candidate with a genuine interest in the process and the constituents was all the change these voters needed.

We made it as easy as possible for them to engage; we listened and told them we would be as helpful as possible if we gained their trust. We didn't promise the world or make broad policy statements. We said we would be present and helpful and try to do the right thing. We built a website with content about the issues of local concern and used email to connect with supporters and to share our ideas.

With a few loyal and hardworking volunteers, and limited financial resources, it boiled down to shoe leather. We knocked on over 10,000 people's front doors, showing them with our actions that we wanted to put them first. If they were not home, we left a card with some basic information on it and then added a handwritten note to personalize our outreach. The simple act of our showing up, smiling, acknowledging their role, and asking for their support was all that many people needed to hear.

I made thousands of phone calls to likely voters who fit our targeted persona. They usually went something like this:

"Hello, my name is Todd Hockenberry, and I am running for Pennsylvania state representative. I am calling to ask for your support."

Silence . . . then a tentative, "Is this really you?"

Everyone assumed I was one of those annoying-as-hell robo-calls that bombard voters in the weeks before an election. When they found out that it was the real live candidate, the content of our message or the rest of the conversation hardly mattered. Most voters were blown away by the fact that I reached out to them in a direct and personal way. I was helping first.

The incumbent hid behind his party's registration advantage and the power of his entrenched party. He employed a defender strategy built on a confidence that was not hard-won or warranted. Our team was honest, engaging, and focused on the persona. The active voter persona concerned with the issues gave us the best chance of victory.

A few weeks before Election Day the state party realized I had a shot to win and we did get a contribution for ads and district-wide mailers, but in the end, I do not believe they were all that convincing or effective. These were the same old interruption marketing techniques that politicians always use and most people ignore. Another piece of junk mail heading straight for the garbage can.

The direct mail campaign that did have an impact was a personal letter from Leanne, my wife. She knew from talking to other women voters that our district needed help. She admitted that she had reluctantly agreed to me running for office because she knew I could make a difference. The postcard was honest, straightforward, without pretense, passionate, and timely, and every word was hers.

I married way over my head.

The result? We lost the election by less than 230 votes, or less than 0.5% of the total voter turnout in the election. We earned a bit less than 50% of the vote with an electorate registered almost 3:1 against the party I represented.

And the main reason we came that close was a relentless focus on our persona.

My opponent relied on the same tactics that had always worked before. Go to the same events, meet the same people, say the same things, and deliver the same "product." Does that sound like anyone (or any businesses) that you know?

Two years later, another candidate ran (I was his campaign manager) and we finally beat the entrenched incumbent. Most of the other local hacks were booted from office, and some were even indicted for corruption. The ringleader went to jail.

We ran our campaign like an inbound organization. Maybe I didn't lose after all.

Chapter 15

Inbound Strategies Match the Buyer's Journey

Stephen Covey said, "Begin with the end in mind."[1] Inbound organizations begin their strategy with the customer in mind.

It may not be obvious but each customer has a unique buying journey. There are similarities, but each person follows a slightly different pace, intensity, breadth, and process before they buy.

Before the onset of inbound marketing in 2007, the buyer journey was primarily a sales journey with most buyers going through a very similar process. In that era, the buyer's journey consisted of salespeople engaging with prospects starting at the beginning of the research phase. Prospective buyers needed to talk to salespeople for preliminary research because salespeople had exclusive access to essential purchasing information. The only way a buyer could thoroughly investigate a solution was to talk with a salesperson.

The salesperson then followed a very defined script and moved the buyer through a structured sales funnel by asking them qualifying questions to determine priority, timeline, budget, and pain. If the buyer met specific criteria, the salesperson would move them to the next stage of the funnel, which typically consisted of a product demo or reviewing a catalog of product features. If the buyer passed through that stage, they entered the answering objections stage, and finally to the defining purchasing terms stage. The salesperson then moved into a closing sequence, pushing the customer to purchase at the salesperson's pace. Once the product sold, the buyer rarely heard from the salesperson again, unless it was a major account that could generate additional revenue with subsequent purchases.

The journey was more about how the sales process applied to the buyer. Understanding the buyer journey was rarely considered as a differentiating factor or competitive advantage. After 2007 this journey became buyer-centric to the point where it no longer resembled a funnel. Now the process is a buyer-controlled 3D amorphous cloud that follows a unique path and cadence with hundreds of variables and bears very little similarity to other buyers and their journeys.

Today, the journey is all about the buyer, and it starts early with online research. One of the guiding principles of inbound is to give value before you extract value. Inbound marketing developed as a philosophy to help companies connect with buyers in this early stage of the process and provide value to searchers as a way of building trust and starting a relationship.

Creating tangible value at every point in the buyer journey makes for a better customer experience. This customer experience becomes the primary influence on the relationship.

Inbound is about recognizing the buyer and their issues and anticipating why, when, and how they buy. The next step as an inbound organization is aligning everyone in every department so that they are prepared to make it easy for prospects to get what they need to start the relationship.

"Customer experience dictates business success these days," says Adam Robinson, VP of marketing at Cerasis.[2]

Rachel Leist, HubSpot's director of marketing new business funnel, says this about buyer journey:

> *Before we make any decision regarding how to nurture our users, we ask if this decision is in the best interests of the customer. We learn from the customer what is in their interest by giving them options to communicate with us like chat, email, phone calls, and our library of content. We gather qualitative research by asking them what they need or want at each stage of the buying journey. We also review quantitative data from the product itself to understand how people are using it. We put ourselves in their shoes to understand from their perspective how our decisions look. We follow the golden rule of inbound marketing—don't market to them in any way we would not want to be marketed to.*[3]

Inbound organizations use technology and automation to make the buyer journey easier and more accessible. A familiar example is using a car-sharing app to find a ride versus the randomness of a cab showing up on the exact street corner at the exact time you need one. Other examples include offering apps, chat, email, and touch-to-dial phone numbers on a website, allowing searchers to connect with you when and how they choose. In the industrial sector, a manufacturer creating a free ROI calculator and buying guide that helps buyers make sense of the purchasing process is another example.

> *Customer experience is . . . the difference between what the customer expects and what the customer gets. Companies that deliver experiences below customer's expectations are disasters, and of course, those that deliver above expectations are winners.*[4]

Inbound organizations deliver a great transaction wrapped in a remarkable customer experience.

The primary general stages of a buyer journey consist of:

+ Awareness
+ Consideration
+ Decision
+ Success

Awareness

The Awareness stage starts when a buyer realizes they have symptoms of a problem and begins looking to find a solution. Buyers begin this stage by discovering a definition for their issues and challenges. They research the source of their particular problem online and start to build ideas of how to solve it. The goal in this stage is to help buyers identify, categorize, and define the problem. At this stage, the buyer is looking for helpful information rather than to complete a purchase.

To get past the Awareness stage, you have to make the short list for vendor consideration. An information exchange drives engagement, and sellers have the opportunity to demonstrate how they work with prospects and customers on an ongoing basis. Remember, 74% of sales go to the first company that was helpful, so your website must be helpful and informative rather than self-serving and product focused.[5]

Buyers may not know exactly what they are looking for in this stage—they know they have an issue, but they may not be clear on the severity, know the potential options for a solution, or know if the problem is even worthwhile to solve. Inbound organizations reach out to their ideal buyer persona contacts and help them ask the right questions. Sometimes the buyer's conclusion in this stage is that they are not ready yet or the issue isn't a major problem and a considered purchase is not a good investment.

Inbound is not all about waiting until someone searches and finds a blog post you wrote about a topic. If you know and understand your persona, if you recognize the issues they face, if you can provide experienced guidance, and if you can add value to their situation, it is acceptable to reach out directly to them and offer to help.

The Awareness stage can last for a long time, sometimes years even for the most basic purchase. Based on economic conditions and business priorities, problems may linger, and buyers stay inactive for long periods of time. Buyers determine when they are ready to move to the next stage and sellers must stand by and support, educate, answer questions, add value, and help until the buyer is ready to move to the next stage. It is counterproductive to force the buyer to move further into the process before they are ready because you risk violating trust. If you skip ahead to the Decision stage, you may lose credibility.

Your website is increasingly the place for buyers to make the first contact or hit the Zero Moment of Truth[6] during the Awareness stage. Almost all consumers (97%) now use online media when researching products and services in their local market and 93% of all B2B purchases start with an Internet search.[7] This increasingly takes place on mobile devices so online assets become critical to starting the relationship process with buyers.

Understanding what triggers your persona to start looking for solutions is also an important part of understanding the buyer journey. A trigger event is an action taken that starts a buying process, such as technology changes, industry disruptions, economic changes, new rules and regulations, competitive pressure, financial moves, employee shake-ups, and product advancements.

In the Awareness stage, buyers are looking to educate themselves, so content should be instructional rather than sales or product oriented. "How to" content—including checklists and "Do you have this problem?" videos are all effective at this stage when you are starting to establish a relationship. Blog posts, e-books, videos, and research-based information have an additional value because they help to attract potential buyers. If you demonstrate that you are an expert or thought leader and create deep and impactful content, you are more likely to get found online. Search engines have evolved to understand the context of search queries and ignore shallow and weak content. Defining your expertise via great content gives you a chance to rise to the top of the massive quantities of content already available online.

Questions you should be able to answer about your target persona in the Awareness stage:

♦ How are potential buyers defining their problems and goals?
♦ What vocabulary do they use to describe them?
♦ Where do they go for information about solving these problems?
♦ What happens if they decide not to pursue a solution?
♦ How do buyers prioritize this problem?

Consideration

In the Consideration stage, buyers know they have a problem and have made progress in defining it. They have identified potential outcomes and begin narrowing options for the type of solutions they will evaluate. In this stage, buyers have usually given a name to the problem or opportunity. They realize there is a wide range of solutions to choose from and they have built a short list of requirements and identified a short list of potential vendors. They may have well-defined decision criteria and a financial budget, decided on a decision process, and figured out a timeframe for getting the problem resolved. Buyers are searching for vendors that have the right expertise to solve their problems in their niche. Buyers in the Consideration stage are moving toward a commitment to change.

Webinars, case studies, demo videos, and Q&A content engage buyers in this stage because they have a better sense of their problem and have whittled down potential solutions; therefore, they are ready for product specific information.

The Consideration stage is an opportunity for the seller to continue to build trust and deepen the relationship. If sellers insist on pushing their specific product or service at this stage and move away from being helpful, they can be eliminated. Buyers are interested in understanding a bit more about why they should consider your solution to solve the problem.

Salespeople help in the Consideration stage by framing the solution in a particular way, asking questions that the buyer didn't consider, running through prerequisites, setting expectations for budget and timeframe for implementation, and leveraging their experience.

Todd tells this story from his time as the vice president of sales and marketing at an industrial laser company:

> *We identified some buyer journey commonalities that we turned into a competitive advantage. In every case, a potential marking laser system buyer asked for a sample of their material marked using our laser. The buyers used these samples to compare the quality of the mark, as well as the competence of the supplier. We realized that this sample was the main selling tool of the engineer or project manager as they were discussing our lasers with the rest of their buying team. As a small company competing against much larger companies, we knew we needed to stand out.*
>
> *Our policy was to return the samples within one working day if at all possible, and overnight ship them back to the buyer. We figured they were asking multiple other laser companies for samples and we wanted to be the first ones with samples back in their hands. We were committed to providing them with a perfect sample and a nice professional report on the equipment and process settings we used to make it.*

This activity won us a lot of business. Our internal process ensured that we knew how to respond to an inquiry for a sample while customizing the response to each buyer. Each laser marking application request was unique, but our process for managing this critical first step in the relationship made a big difference through the rest of the buyer's journey.

As buyers transition from Awareness to Consideration, inbound organizations have to make tough decisions about whether the buyer is a good fit. Persona information becomes critical to making that assessment. In the pre-2007 era, sellers sold to everyone. Today, an inbound organization is very selective in the type, size, and attributes of good fit buyers and sets the right expectations to ensure a better and happy customer base. Telling a client you are not a good fit is hard, but it's the best thing for both parties involved. Committing to a niche and an ideal buyer persona makes it easy for you to create a reputation for honesty, trust, and effectiveness, potentially leading to more business.

Questions you should be able to answer about your target persona in the Consideration stage:

- ♦ What types of options do buyers have for different categories of solutions?
- ♦ Where do buyers go for information about these options?
- ♦ What are the advantages and weaknesses of each option?
- ♦ What factors do buyers weigh most heavily when deciding which option to choose?
- ♦ What are the objections for each solution category?

Decision

In the Decision stage, buyers have determined the type of solution or method they want to pursue and are evaluating the specific buying options that are available. Buyers have narrowed down the choices and determined the final options, including a short list of potential vendors. Buyers are comparing the best two or three alternatives, testing them, and planning for implementation.

When buyers move to the Decision stage, they are deciding on the specific vendor and solution options and comparing them against one another to determine which one is the best to help solve their problem. Free trials, proposals, consultations with experts, and references are influential at this stage. If you have created engagement and built credibility through the early stages of the process, you are now in a position to make a compelling offer that moves the buyer to a decision.

Questions you should be able to answer about your target persona in the Decision stage:

- Do we understand who this buyer is and what they need?
- Are they a good fit for our solution?
- Would this buyer make a great customer?
- Do we understand the problem, goals, plans, challenges, and timeline?
- Do we understand the decision process and decision criteria?
- What are the barriers to making a decision?

Once a buyer decides on the specific solution and selects a vendor, the Success stage begins. Now a seller concentrates on solving the problem. They move their relationships from vendor to the preferred supplier and, hopefully, from partner to trusted advisor.

Success

Inbound success has one job: to make sure buyers are ultimately successful solving the problem that they originally defined.

Today, success is defined in terms of the buyer's goals and expectations. It is developed during the Consideration and Decision stages. The goal of the Success stage is to keep the customer so happy that they become a reference and then an advocate for your company and solution.

Inbound organizations create post-sale content designed to drive customer success starting with account set-up and installation. They invest in training videos and instructor-led webinars or training, onboarding help, project plans, frequently asked questions lists, periodic update reviews, surveys, and customer support. Effective inbound success programs reinforce the buyer's decision and deepen their relationship with your organization by driving their success. Once the buyer is through the initial launch phase, content should be focused on helping the buyer get the most from their solution.

Questions you should be able to answer about your target persona in the Success stage:

♦ How do we make onboarding, installation, and implementation easier?
♦ How do we provide ever-increasing, ongoing value?
♦ What related problems do we solve that would enhance the relationship?

Inbound organizations understand the details of the buyer journey, map it, and use that knowledge to design a customer experience that the target persona loves. Creating inbound strategies that solve for the customer at all points in the buyer journey creates a competitive advantage.

Once you have determined your inbound strategies at each stage of the buyer journey you then develop plays to implement them. MSPOT plays describe the detailed projects required to execute the strategies.

To Do

☐ Define the buyer journey.

☐ What events trigger a reaction by your target persona to change?

☐ List the most effective marketing and sales touch-points that lead to engagement.

☐ Outline the key decisions your buyer persona makes at each stage of the journey.

☐ Build and share the journey map and use it to guide your MSPOT action plans.

Chapter 16

Centralized View of the Customer

For teams to make decisions closest to the customer, they need to have access to the right historical data. A centralized view of the customer is a single record for every contact. It includes each event or interaction a connection has with the organization. All contacts with the people or content from marketing, sales, service, and operations become the data archive of your organization's relationship with that person.

A centralized view of the customer allows an inbound team to have access to essential transaction data and product status. It will enable your team to develop insights into the contact's behavior, issues, interests, and needs. These data insights guide the creation of an action plan designed to engage and help each customer.

A centralized view of the customer improves your relationship because response and decision-making time are faster and more comprehensive. Interactions become personalized with individual requests and preferences, and it is easier for employees to identify previous potholes and subjects to avoid. The centralized view of the customer helps take complex information and makes it simple so the team can make decisions and take action.

When the data about your customer is in one place, you have the potential to analyze it and take action. From this comes insights into your customer's activities and personal preferences. Your customer-facing teams can be proactive, anticipating what customers might need in the future. A centralized view gives you the best chance to provide the right help at the right time to your target persona as they progress along the buyer journey.

Pete Caputa, CEO of Databox, talks about the centralized view of the customer:

> *Most companies are incessantly pushing their products and solutions to every prospect and customer in the same way because that's what they've always done. But, this approach is getting more and more expensive and less and less effective as buyers get accustomed to Amazon-like experiences.*
>
> *In contrast, inbound organizations are leading their prospects and customers to the right spot at the right time via the right communication channels.*
>
> *The goal of an inbound organization is to understand what each customer is trying to accomplish, so marketing sends the right message, sales tailors their approach, and customer service can make custom, context-aware recommendations.*
>
> *Every marketing touchpoint should be personalized and targeted instead of mass-blasted. Sales must be focused on discovering and advising, instead of hounding and pitching. Service should know exactly why the customer bought and what success looks like for them instead of relying on scripted processes that end no matter what results a customer gets.*
>
> *The first and last step of accomplishing this change is the creation of a centralized view of every customer, so sales, marketing, and services teams can see what each other is doing.*[1]

Warning

How do you build a centralized view of the customer without imposing centralized control of the customer relationship and experience?

The answer lies in the way your team uses information and how it relates to your mission and culture. Centralized control can lead to overbearing processes that result in slow decision making. A centralized view of the customer accelerates decision making because it provides essential information to the employees that engage with customers on a daily basis.

By unifying the view of the customer, you empower employees to act within the culture to execute on your organization's mission. Leaders and managers should provide the right tools and automation for customer-facing employees. The creation and maintenance of the centralized view of the customer is a primary focus of the organization and must be accessible to update or modify, and user friendly.

The key is a balance. Centralize the platform and decentralize the decisions that enhance customer's experience.

How to Build a Centralized View of the Customer

To build a centralized view of the customer, start with a modern technology stack that has the basics: cloud based, easy to implement, easy to install, and easy for individuals to use. Legacy technology systems are sometimes deployed in a siloed format, based on the entrepreneurial needs of a growing company. When each department uses a different tool, it creates a disjointed process: one group may have access to the information they need, but everyone else faces barriers.

Creating a centralized view of the customer is hard. A good first step is to deploy a technology stack that unifies the marketing, sales, and service views of the customer.

Tools like HubSpot software combine all these components, including CRM, marketing automation, and service management, in one place. Each customer record is accessible by all customer-facing teams to track each interaction with each individual contact from the very first touch. This includes the first visit to your website and which pages are viewed, session times, and the last page viewed. Email sends, opens, and click-throughs are added to the contact timeline as well as meetings, phone calls, check-in calls, customer support calls, all marketing communications, sales interactions, and service requests. Qualitative and quantitative data are mapped to the buyer journey. This includes site visits, conversions, blog views, social media shares/likes, content engagement, chat, messaging, and meetings. This one centralized view allows your team to understand what they need to be successful.

A modern CRM, connected to marketing automation tools, provides important data needed to analyze buying patterns, presale behavior, responses to offers, engagement with content, personal communications with your team, and other data points from each touch with the customer.

Today, using spreadsheets and email tools to manage customer relationships puts businesses at a disadvantage. Over half of all SMBs' enterprises use manual methods, like spreadsheets and whiteboards, to keep track of customers. Tracking in this fashion is inefficient, subject to human error, and creates dangerous silos. The inability to access customer information can lead to customers that are annoyed and disappointed. They may choose to find a company considerate enough to invest in tools that give them better answers.

Everyone has had this agonizing experience: you are forced to call customer support and are handed off seven times to seven different people, and they all ask you for the same basic, but redundant, information. This signals a lack of a centralized view of the customer and is wasteful and frustrating, and puts the relationship at risk.

A centralized view of the customer allows your team to deliver a great customer experience that builds loyalty, creates brand advocacy, and grows your revenue. A recent study shows that 75% of sales managers say that using a CRM helps them increase sales, and companies who invest in a CRM generate over five times the return on their investment.[2]

A centralized view of the customer gives your team an important advantage to help you build deep engagement; measure, analyze, and better understand the buyer journey; and create long-term customer relationships.

To Do

- ☐ Assess your current tools used to track customer data and interactions.
- ☐ Choose a modern CRM that will help you keep track of all prospect and customer interactions.
- ☐ Create a centralized view of the customer for your team.
- ☐ Begin gathering data and developing insights.

Chapter 17

My Car Dealer, No Help at All

Todd tells this story about his experience with a dealership for one of the world's largest automotive companies.

Three years ago, I bought a new car, and after the car was purchased the dealership worked hard to keep me coming back for warranty service and maintenance. The service team was professional, friendly, and helpful. Right around the three-year anniversary of the purchase, I started getting calls from the dealer asking if I wanted to sell my car, since supposedly "there was high demand for my make and model" on the used car market.

I'm a buy-and-hold kind of guy when it comes to cars; I drove my last car 250,000 miles. I buy them, I service them correctly, and I keep them as long as they run reliably. This car was only three years old, and I figured I would own it for another 10 years. However, the dealership called me at least once a month for four months trying to get me to sell that car. It wasn't one inquiry, it was multiple calls every month, and those calls kept coming

Each time they called, I politely told them, "Please make a note in your CRM. You have a CRM, right?" They said, "Yes." I tried to be as explicit as possible. "Please make a note in your CRM that I am not going to sell this car anytime soon. Please do not call me again and ask me if I want to trade it in."

On the fifth such call, I was a little less patient. "This is getting ridiculous," I said. "If you call me again, I promise you, I will never step foot within your dealership again. Ever. For anything. For the rest of my life."

Guess what happened the next month? The dealership called me again. I said, "That's it. I warned you. You didn't listen. You neglected to put the notes in my contact record to not call me, so I am never coming back to your dealership. I will never buy anything from you again."

I said, "I hope you're recording this call and your management hears it." Sure enough, they were recording the call. The boss called me an hour later. She was apologetic in every way, up and down, trying to explain the circumstances.

Her proposed solution to make me happy again was to remove my name from the database so that none of the dealership employees could even attempt to call me. Even that solution did not work. They called me again with the same pitch less than three months later.

The manager was very pleasant and considerate. She said she was going to send me a little something to make it up to me, a certificate for some free service. But I told her it wasn't good enough. I had already warned the dealership contacts who called me the previous four times. Now, six times in total. The time for a discount to make me happy had long passed. The customer service follow-up staff had betrayed the trust built over the previous three years since the initial sale. I was happy with them. I had no outstanding issues. I loved driving that vehicle. The dealership performed great service when I brought the car for warranty service on the recommended schedule. But their service marketing follow-up ruined it all. The positive experience of a multiyear relationship went out the window, and now I had moved on. Another dealer services the vehicle.

The dealer's service follow-up was completely out of sync with my persona, my buyer journey, and me.

The lesson for businesses today is that mistakes like this ruin the entire buyer experience and can end the relationship. The buyer is in control, has options, and no longer has to tolerate a bad experience.

Let's review this example through the lens of an ideal inbound strategy.

Was this part of the customer experience personalized to the buyer?

No. Our family owns another vehicle from another car company, and they run the same service promotion, so it was disingenuous. The other dealership had a better CRM and stopped calling after I explained our buy-and-hold philosophy. At the first dealership, I wasn't treated with honesty or respect. I was treated like a box to check or a rule to follow. They didn't even listen to me.

Was the dealership engaging?

No. They talked and never listened. When I picked up the phone, the rep went straight to the pitch and didn't ask me any questions about what I wanted and how I wanted to be treated. They had no interest in helping me with my particular situation. Even when I stated my preference, they didn't take the extra step to try to help; they ignored my request.

Was this interaction layered to match where I was on the buyer journey?

Not at all. The rep wanted to push me into his "three years since the sale" bucket and get another call in. He had no way to differentiate me from the other three-year buyers or acknowledge my preferences. The service department couldn't differentiate between different types of customers and was under the mistaken impression that everyone who buys a car would want to upgrade three years later. They arrogantly believed they could push everyone into one bucket and provide the same experience to everyone, regardless of my stated preference.

Was the service interaction human?

Nope. The dealership had no interest in developing an understanding of me as a person or treating me like a human being. Would they ask me the same question five times if I were standing in front of them? There was no interest in establishing a personal relationship with me or acknowledging and accepting my car buying habits. At best, I was a transaction even when I stated my personal preference. I told them many times I was the buy-and-hold persona. How hard would it have been to have a script or playbook that pivoted into another offer for special service for buy-and-hold people? How hard would it have been to provide me educational content that explained how to maintain my vehicle to reach maximum miles driven? Maybe even a concierge service for people who make a long-term commitment to servicing the vehicle exclusively at that dealer for the life of the car. The fact that I was three years post-purchase mattered much more to them than treating me like a human being.

Are my expectations are too high for a car dealership? No way. I spent a lot of money with them and committed to their product for the long term. Shouldn't I expect a reciprocal arrangement if I drop $45,000?

What produced this experience?

The service reps probably had a quota of calls to make, maybe 120 a day. They were using an auto dialer and started off each call by annoying me since no one likes that pause, click, noise in the background, and then someone finally picks up. They were burdened with lousy information systems that provided no way to systematically notate my preferences once they found out I was the buy-and-hold persona. The last rep who called me had no context from the previous calls or feedback I shared, so he was at a decided disadvantage. He was not empowered to engage with me beyond the narrow offer of getting me to trade in my car for a new one.

The manager who called probably used a natural language processing tool to understand that they had an issue with a customer, and she jumped in to take over for the service rep and try to stop the bleeding the best she could. Her proposed solution to make me happy by taking me out of the database indicates that there was no internal mechanism to improve the experience for customers.

Neither the manager nor the service rep were empowered to engage me or make a real decision, resulting in a negative experience that led to a death spiral for our relationship.

It is easy to imagine a sterile, corporate environment with rows and rows of desks with unhappy people wearing headsets making their calls with the sole intent of hitting their dialing numbers. The dealership team lacked the culture, the systems, the processes, and the leadership needed to deliver a positive customer experience that I as a buyer desire and expect.

The problem is not with the employees in the trenches who make the calls, but with the leaders of companies that still think this type of service process is a valuable activity. When you treat all your customers the same and ignore the reality of today's buyer, you potentially reverse all of the goodwill the marketing, sales, and service teams and the rest of the company created.

This is not an inbound organization.

Chapter 18

Inbound Marketing Is a Strategic Imperative

Inbound marketing is a strategy focused on attracting buyer attention by using relevant and helpful content. By matching content to every stage of the buying journey, a seller can add value to every interaction. Potential buyers find, research, and select potential vendors through channels like blogs, online events, search engines, email, and social media and move at their own pace toward a purchasing decision.

Inbound marketing is about creating poignant, personalized content to address the problems and needs of the ideal buyer personas, and then attracting those prospects online to earn their trust and gain their business. Inbound marketing isn't about blasting the same message to everyone as if using a bullhorn. It doesn't try to interrupt people to get their attention. Inbound marketing is about being human, adding value before extracting value, and providing help for buyers who need it.

Because the content is the primary vehicle buyers use to find answers to their questions and to solve their problems, online content becomes strategic in helping prospects make decisions as they move through the stages of the buyer journey.

Why Inbound Organizations Must Be Great at Producing and Publishing Content

Because 97% of consumers now use online media when researching products and services in their local market[1] and 93% of all B2B purchases start with an Internet search,[2] inbound marketing should be a priority if organizations want to reach consumers.

Content is the tangible output of the information defined in your inbound strategy, translated into a format buyers find, consume, and review—like an e-book, white paper, checklist, video, podcast, SlideShare, social media post, or blog article. Content should contain your experience and expertise packaged in a digestible format, available throughout your website and designed to help anyone who is interested. Prospects consume this material as they research, understand, frame, and move toward a solution to their problem. Inbound marketing is the strategy your organization employs to get your content found and to engage with buyers at each stage of the funnel.

It is vital for business leaders to understand the role content plays in this process. Content should be consistent with the company mission and vision and reflective of organizational values. Paying attention to content is as important as the overall company brand.

Adam Robinson, marketing director of Cerasis, puts the connection between leaders, leadership, and content this way: "Content leadership typically builds trust and extends to being seen as a leader in other aspects of your business. If we're seen as a leader in content, the perception is most likely that we're a leader in the services and the technology that we provide."[3]

What Is the Source of Great Content?

Great content comes from an organization thinking about things deeply and clearly. "Writing is thinking. To write well is to think clearly. That's why it's so hard."[4]

"The value people get from your content is related to the amount of thought you put into it. People are busy, we don't always have time to think deeply about our work and how to be better—that's what great content does, it does the hard work of thinking for us," says Janessa Lantz, a HubSpot senior marketing manager.[5]

What should your organization be thinking about? The primary focus should be on the issues that cause the ideal buyer persona to struggle. It may not be a specific, narrow technical problem, but you should be thinking about the buyer in the context of their world, the strategic issues, and barriers to success that they face on a daily basis. Great content comes from taking a specific subject, making it easy to digest and understand, communicating your ideas to the audience, and providing a guide that directs them to take some form of action that can help.

Why do you need to define the problems buyers want to solve, rather than describe the products that you want to sell? Because buyers want a solution, an answer; they want the feeling that comes with addressing the issue and getting a good outcome. They don't care about your product. Buyers need to know you offer something more than the products and services in your product catalog or rate card. Content is a way to share this knowledge in a form that is helpful to them. Great buyer-focused content means eliminating self-serving, vacuous, marketing-speak like "We have excellent customer service," or "We are consultative." It involves creating content with industry vocabulary that makes it easy to understand.

Content is strategic because it affects nearly every aspect of the buyer journey. There are no shortcuts to building great content.

Inbound marketing strategy is built on a series of plays and tactics including SEO, social media, email, analytics, inbound links, comments, landing pages, workflows, and other mechanisms for making your expertise expressed in content findable by your buyer.

A core principle of inbound content is to attract instead of to interrupt, strategically placing content where your best prospects are looking for information as they educate themselves about their situations and possible paths to improvement. Search engines favor actual experts and expertise over generic bulk-produced content.

Andrew Quinn talks about the sources of content:

> *The first thing is to start looking at your customers and your prospects and who they are and what do they care about. Why do they choose us? What are the choices they can make? What decisions are they making? And why do they make them? With this understanding, you can create highly valuable answers that they will then find. And that's an incredibly effective use of your business's time and your money.*[6]

What Are the Most Important Types of Content to Produce?

Content is the essence of your expertise, communicated in a way that your audience understands and absorbs the message. It helps them improve their situation by moving them to their desired end state.

- **Application Content**—describes how, when, and where a product or service is used, including industry or user-focused information. Application content shows how to use the product in a particular circumstance and the outcomes that will result from that use.
- **Solution Content**—describes why this solution is the best way to address the problem, frequently in Q&A form. It is easy to understand, shows mastery of the problem, and makes it easy for prospects to see different options.

- **Outcome Content**—shows the specific path from problem identification to goal achievement, starting with the goal and working backward, while outlining a complete way to get there.
- **Persona Content**—provides information focused on a particular personality, role, or position and how to make their life better, more comfortable, or faster. Also gives any other details on outcomes they wish to achieve.
- **Insight Content**—delivers actionable intelligence derived from research that helps the reader make sense of their world. Analysis of industries, strategy, data, or technology trends.
- **Product/Service Content**—includes features, specifications, and technical details. This is often the first thing organizations work on when it comes to content and, in most cases, this is the least relevant and exciting content to the buyer.

Even if you choose to outsource content creation, your top subject matter experts need to be involved.

Janessa Lantz says this about creating content:

You can't expect to bring in a young, inexperienced recent college graduate and expect them to be good at creating content. That person, or someone like them, can create a blog schedule and create low-value content to check the box for meeting a schedule, but that is not how successful content works anymore. If you create one great piece of content, you get a hundred times the results, as measured in engagement and interest, than if you create one hundred pieces of mediocre content.[7]

Inbound organizations understand how important content is to communicate the mission, culture, and strategies for both internal and external consumption.

The Secret of a Successful Inbound Marketing and Content Strategy

A recent Content Marketing Institute survey[8] found the following:

- 88% of B2B respondents say their organization uses content marketing.
- Only 30% say their organization's content is effective or accomplishes their overall objectives.
- Only 44% said their organization is clear on what an effective content marketing program even looks like.
- 32% said they had a documented content marketing strategy.

If almost 9 out of 10 companies use content, why are so few successful at it?

The most significant barrier to a successful inbound marketing and content strategy is the disconnect between the buyer's interest and the marketer's offering. Organizations that take a strategic approach create content that starts with the buyer and works backward. Organizations that produce product- and feature-focused content are less successful.

The buyer must be front and center in all inbound marketing content efforts. If you develop the ideal buyer persona and use it to guide inbound marketing and content development, you will get better results. If you are not helping your persona, but are pitching and selling products, then your inbound marketing efforts will fail.

Buyers smell insincerity a mile away. A recent study by Google showed that visitors make first impressions of your website in as little as half a second and it takes 2.6 seconds to find the most critical elements on a site that focus their attention. The research further showed that websites with simple designs or low complexity as well as a familiar layout were highly preferred by visitors. Being straightforward in your messaging and presenting your content in ways familiar to your persona leads to trust.

Buyers focus on content that is engaging. Engaging means they are paying attention to the content and learning from it. Content that is boring, uninteresting, or hard to navigate will lose the reader and might very well create a negative impression of your brand. Great content flows from effective persona work, the questions the buyers ask, and your honesty and expertise in answering them.

Once you create great content, you still need to present it in a way that is interesting. Great content is different from writing an academic or technical paper. The presentation of content needs to assist in driving deeper engagement by informing, educating, and even entertaining your ideal buyer persona.

Today's buyer wants the relationship to be personal, so content must be personalized. Content is the link, the glue, the connection between you and your potential customer. Even when your sales team or service people are engaging with customers, content will be a large part of the ongoing experience.

Personalization is an excellent place to start. Emails with the recipient's name, web pages that recognize your IP address, appropriate call-to-action graphics, and customized landing pages help build a better relationship. Using common vocabulary, determining communication preferences (text, email, or phone), and figuring out optimal frequency impact your message.

Combining personalization with the appropriate content for each phase of the buying journey enhances the relationship. Delivering customized experiences (HubSpot calls this *smart content*) allows companies to be more helpful. This method of producing unique content will become the standard as new technologies emerge.

An excellent example of personalization is the music provider Spotify. The more you use the product, the more personal the music becomes. Spotify uses your listening behavior to serve you even more great content. No one can listen to every artist, so Spotify uses your stated preferences as well as what you listen to and makes recommendations. Spotify uses data to make your relationship more personal by sending weekly favorites to your playlists. Your Spotify playlist is like no one else's. It is very individual and personalized.

Content must be layered across the buyer journey and used by the people on your team who are communicating with the buyer. Marketing departments should be able to see statistics about which content gets opened the most frequently and when. Aggregating the results allows marketing and sales people to understand the best material to deploy at the best time and match the stage of the buyer with the right content via a content library with modularity, sorted based on the persona, industry, specific buyer stage, topic, and business outcome.

For example, creating a video that addresses the multiple types of competitive solution categories used by your three personas gives you maximum flexibility. This video could appear in blog posts, site pages, and emails to different target personas along with text that describes the outcome of using your solution in a particular application.

Building a matrix of content gives you the flexibility to apply the right material to the proper situation, delivering a personal experience for your buyer. The goal of strategic content is to provide buyers and influencers the ammunition they need to advance their decision making. Content fills the gaps between the personal interactions with your company.

Inbound organizations use content strategically and match the right content to the right persona at the right time in the proper stage. If the content is product focused, generalized, laden with marketing jargon, dull, or dated, buyers will ignore it. In today's buying environment, that means they ignore you too.

What You Get from Inbound Marketing and Content

Inbound marketing drives measurable results:

- ◆ Target prospects find your content online.
- ◆ Prospects engage earlier in buyer journey via education offers.
- ◆ Relationships become focused on helping, which builds trust.
- ◆ Better engagement with buyers improves the buying process.
- ◆ A better customer experience is delivered.
- ◆ Your reputation as a thought leader improves.
- ◆ More leads are generated, lowering acquisition costs.
- ◆ Net new customers and revenue growth increase.

Content and content marketing evolve all the time. Technology is moving fast, and buyers are moving even quicker because they rely on content to stay up to date. Every day more content is consumed using mobile devices. AI is starting to drive content creation, distribution, and personalization. These trends are vital reasons businesses need to think of content as a strategic question.

Chatbots, influencer marketing, even paid ads and sponsored promotion depend on great content. The trends point to persona-based, helpful content as being necessary for any new promotion and distribution channels for inbound marketing in the future.

The concepts defined in this chapter regarding external content hold true for content created for internal uses as well. One of the critical characteristics of the organizations we studied is that they use the same approach internally to educate and inform employees, partners, and suppliers. Content supports every educational initiative both internally and externally in the organization's ecosystem. An inbound organization leans on strategic content as the foundation for helping first.

The most important part of creating strategic content is that you must have something important to share, something to contribute to the conversation in your world, something that is worthwhile to read. Organizations that fail to see the connection between their thinking and the buyer's problems frequently struggle. Inbound organizations should be great content producers and promoters to everyone in their ecosystem.

Justin Champion, author of *Inbound Content: A Step-by-Step Guide to Doing Content Marketing the Inbound Way*, puts it this way, "If your goal is to create content that attracts, converts, closes, and delights your ideal customers, then you need the commitment, excitement, and dedication of your entire company to make it happen."[9]

Inbound marketing is not a short-term play or quick fix. You can't start it one week and pause it the next. Success depends on a long-term commitment to inbound marketing as a core organizational strategy with the appropriate focus, resources, and patience required of any other sizeable strategic initiative.

To Do

☐ Conduct a content audit to understand trends.
☐ Chart content assets and review the gaps.
☐ Map content to the persona's buyer journey.
☐ Create new strategic content for each step in the buyer's journey.

Chapter 19

Bell Performance—Content Attracting, Engaging, and Helping an Audience

How do you rebuild a company that is over 100 years old, has lost its charismatic CEO, experienced significant turnover in the sales channel, and is led by a young and untested leadership team?

You build an inbound organization.

Thirty-year-old Glenn Williams faced the above scenario with an added twist; his father was the leader who passed away far too soon and left him to guide the family company and reputation.

Williams did have several advantages. He knew the industry and target market very well, having been a part of Bell Performance for many years. He also knew that the world of fuel additives is frequently perceived as an industry dominated by unethical companies who sell snake oil and push dubious claims and sometimes shady products.

There is general uncertainty among consumers about what a fuel additive is, what it does, and when it is appropriate to use one. Williams understood this market dynamic better than anyone because Bell Performance invented the fuel additive market back in 1909.

Glenn decided that to achieve success, he needed to change the general perception of the fuel additives industry. He needed to help both B2C and B2B buyers cut through the fluff and address the confusion once and for all. He decided to make Bell Performance the most helpful brand in its market by providing education, information, and evidence for every claim made about fuel additives. He decided to execute a strategy built on the idea of helping buyers first to understand the causes of engine issues, and then offer fuel additives as a way to fix the problem.

Before Glenn took over, Bell Performance relied on a sales and marketing strategy that leveraged small, independent distributors who each covered a specific geographic area. Each distributor was responsible for moving a small quantity of product every year. This distribution model was somewhat inefficient and started to run out of steam through the 1990s. It came to a full stop once the management team who built this network on personal relationships was no longer active.

Under Glenn's direction, Bell decided to advance the educational strategy on their website. He also decided to build a brand new B2B distribution network to use a more effective sales process and take better advantage of the changes in buyer behavior he had observed.

Bell's challenges relating to their digital marketing strategy are common to many traditional companies. Bell outsourced the management of the website to an IT provider and had no direct control over the content, optimization, or results. Making changes to the website was a costly and time-consuming process. Bell had a website because they needed an online brochure. It wasn't strategic, and it certainly wasn't generating any revenue.

Glenn realized there was an opportunity to generate leads directly from B2C buyers and cultivate interest from select B2B companies using this education-oriented target approach.

Bell rebuilt their sales and marketing team around this strategy. They hired experts in engine and fuel technology; they added inside salespeople to support the distribution network (as opposed to people in the field who spent a lot of time driving to visit customers). They dedicated significant time and content to understanding the issues with engines affected by fuel and helped by fuel additives. The team learned how to convert their expertise into content that could be shared and consumed by the target audience that needed it.

Bell assembled their people into teams that aligned with the target buyers and let each team follow the customer through the entire buying journey. Everyone at Bell learned the details of the buyer persona, what the expectations are of that persona at each stage in the buyer journey, how to be helpful to start and not pushy to get a quick transaction, and their role in delivering the best fuel additive solutions to each customer.

Glenn Williams describes the company's focus:

Our goal was, and still is, to create a significant online presence that generates sales revenue, educates consumers and businesses, and convinces them to allow us to help them with their fuel-related issues. We wanted to expand our influence and increase the number of people that knew about Bell. We achieved those goals by building a marketing platform and content development process that allowed us to create amazing content that continues to expand our presence online and support our sales team as they build relationships and work with our customers to solve their problems. The focus on educating and helping is a different experience for Bell buyers. They come away from our website feeling that they received the helpful information they needed as well as a proven product to improve their engine's performance. And then our employees reinforce that feeling.[1]

Bell adopted an inbound marketing strategy eight years ago, in 2010. Back in that era, fuel additive companies fought for shelf space in automotive supply stores, big box retailers, or specialty stores to service vertical markets like boating or trucking service. Bell decided to focus on two markets: the end user who was motivated to buy directly from the industry leader and distributors outside of the traditional retail model. Bell understood the changes in buyer behavior toward favoring more online research and chose to become the magnet that attracted that type of buyer.

Erik Bjornstad, Bell Performance product manager, describes this shift:

> Inbound marketing powered by HubSpot allowed us to differentiate ourselves from our much-larger and more resourced competitors. Our competitors don't have focused strategies centered on the topics that consumers and businesses are looking for. Even the large national brands we compete with focus on the product and not the persona. We do that routinely, and the benefits have been significant.[2]

Bell developed, and often updates, specific personas for both B2B and B2C buyers. Bjornstad continues:

> There are unique attributes of B2C buyers of fuel additives. Not everyone uses these products because not everyone has issues with their fuel. We target consumers that are very particular about their engines and engine performance. We also understand and help specific businesses that have mission critical functions that are affected when faced with fuel related problems, such as bacteria accumulating in a diesel fuel tank used for a backup generator at a hospital.[3]

A core part of the Bell content strategy is a blog on their company website. Bell has a separate blog for each of their high-level personas: one for the B2C end user and one for the B2B business buyer. The consumer blog focuses on fuel and engine issues for cars, classic vehicles, boats, jet skis, motorcycles, small equipment, generators, and home heating. The business blog deals with fuel storage, fleet management, heavy trucks, power plants, large backup generators, and other engines used in and by companies. Each blog focuses on solving the problems that those end users have every day.

Starting from zero blog traffic and less than 500 unique site visits per month in 2010, Bell has grown their online traffic to over 175,000 visits per month with over 90% of those visits starting their journey by reading a blog post. Bell's blog posts are often given primary status by Google as the featured snippet for the topic, further broadening their reach.

Bell continues to keep their content fresh by answering buyers' questions and adds blog posts to inform the readers about new product updates, the impact of additives on new engines, and checklists for getting a better ROI. Many of their posts are now ranked number one for a specific search topic and have remained at the top of the rankings for many years. These anchor posts drive increasing amounts of traffic month over month.

Williams describes the impact of his company's blog:

> *Our top performing blog posts are an asset to the company, and we view them that way. These posts drive new traffic, convert visitors to leads, and drive product sales to our online store. The key is to make sure we always keep the customer in the front of our mind when we are creating content and talk to them like we are talking to one of our friends or a customer who we met at a retail store. Helpful, informative, honest, and clear.*[4]

Bell publishes other strategic content including e-books, infographics, videos, and white papers all designed to follow the same process. Bell takes their engineering and technical expertise and translates that asset into actionable content and suggestions that the reader uses immediately.

"Fuel and engine performance is complicated and filled with incomprehensible technical detail. Our job is to take the complex, make it straightforward, and provide evidence based on fact and data that our solutions deliver superior performance and solve the issues our customers deal with every day," says Williams.[5]

Bell knows that adding a new product line is an investment for a distributor. To help them understand the opportunity, Bell creates unique content to educate prospective distributors. The content for distributors focuses on the ideal target markets needing Bell's help, the personas that best fit the Bell solutions, as well as specific content for onboarding, training, and support of distributor teams. Bell shares customer success stories, so distributors learn how best to approach their marketplace. Bell encourages distributors to engage with them through their blog and social media so that they stay connected and informed.

Few companies can say the words "since 1909," but Bell Performance does. Since that very first day, they have pursued a vision summed up like this: "May the world be better, because of Bell Performance."

Inbound marketing and sales are helping Bell extend their reach and improve the understanding of people struggling with fuel-related engine issues all over the world.

Bell Performance is an inbound organization.

Chapter 20

Inbound Selling

Inbound selling takes the inbound philosophy and integrates it into a modern sales process to deliver a superior buying experience. Inbound salespeople are respectful, friendly, and human, and focus on helping first. They listen to buyer feedback, make thoughtful recommendations, and leverage strategic content to provide the right information at the right time. They are careful to move at the buyer's pace and look to create a long-term relationship with good fit customers.

Two key ideas define inbound selling: (1) inbound sales teams base their entire strategy on coordinating the buyer journey, and (2) inbound sales teams deliver information in the buyer's context and personalize the whole sales experience, rather than running the same sales process for everyone.

Table 20.1 shows some of the significant differences between traditional sales and inbound sales.

Inbound marketing became popular more than 10 years ago, because modern marketers recognized the new era of buyer behavior and wanted to change traditional marketing tactics and treat buyers more like human beings. Unfortunately, salespeople were slow to take advantage of this evolution. Instead of modifying the sales process to accommodate buyer control, most salespeople kept doing what they had always done.

TABLE 20.1   Differences between Sales Techniques

Traditional	Inbound Sales
Sells to all companies	Works primarily with the ideal buyer profile
Sells to everybody	Works primarily with targeted buyer personas
Calls all leads	Prioritizes leads that are close to the Consideration and Decision stages
Asks questions about research history	Reviews lead intelligence, lead notifications, and previous contact history based on available data
Calls and leaves one message—sends one email to get in touch	Creates value-added outreach and engages multiple times to make a connection
Treats all prospects like they are in the same buying phase	Treats prospects differently based on where they are in the buying process
Qualifies a prospect on the first interaction	Offers to help on the first interaction
Gives references at the end of the sales process	Provides references at the beginning of the buyer journey
Tells you what you need	Listens to understand what you want
Quickly moves to a product demonstration	Leads a discovery call or meeting to understand the customer's specific needs
Wants to talk to a decision maker	Works with a group of decision influencers
Wants to connect face-to-face	Prefers to connect via video conferencing
Relies on discounts to close deals	Relies on product fit and value while understanding price is important
Closes the deal and moves to the next one	Stays active in account management throughout the customer relationship
Tells people how to buy	Explains the best way to get started
Leverages personal referrals	Uses social media to expand thought leadership and generate interest

Regardless of the difficulty getting buyers to return calls, reply to an email, meet in person, and move deals quickly, most salespeople continued to struggle along the same path. In 2012, a few early adopters saw an opportunity to leverage the inbound philosophy and started to use inbound sales techniques to differentiate the way they connected to prospects. They understood that a large percentage of a buyer's journey was being conducted before a salesperson became involved. They decided to offer free help, post educational content, leverage social media for effective outreach, learn the ideal buyer persona, study the best material to deliver at each stage of the buyer journey, prioritize specific opportunities, and act as consultants. They also decided to treat everyone differently, personalize the sales process, and, most importantly, give the buyer control.

In 2015, Dan wrote a blog article, "Always Be Closing Is Dead: How to Always Be Helping," which described the impact that inbound has on the sales process.[1] Today, we know the inbound sales process works. It creates a superior customer experience for the buyer, helps build a large pool of available prospects for the seller, and is a key factor in helping salespeople exceed their quota.

What does inbound selling mean for a business owner or CEO?

If your sales reps are still using a traditional sales playbook, you may be frustrating your prospects and customers. That could have a more significant impact than it did 10 years ago. In the old days, an overly aggressive salesperson received a nasty letter from a customer or a call from his sales manager telling him to knock it off, then went back and duplicated the process with the next prospect. Today, frustrated buyers post their thoughts and ideas on social media for the entire world to see. Salespeople live and die by their company's online reputation.

Inbound selling also improves sales productivity by eliminating a lot of the low-value activities that take up a lot of your salespeople's time. Inbound sales teams spend most of their time talking with leads who have already shown interest in moving closer to a decision. While traditional salespeople are responsible for talking to everyone, inbound salespeople speak with prospects who have expressed an interest in learning more.

Inbound salespeople talk with more prospects than traditional salespeople do because they use technology to manage automated tasks like follow-up emails and booking meetings, sending out customized proposals, and adding lead intelligence to their CRM. Inbound salespeople dig deep into customer problems through a discovery process rather than showing a product demo. Inbound salespeople use social media to generate a wide audience, connect good fit prospects at the top of the funnel so they can collaborate, and deliver strategic content to the right part of the sales process.

Brian Signorelli, author of *Inbound Selling: How to Change the Way You Sell to Match How People Buy*, says:

> *Inbound selling is a modern, buyer-centric form of sales where the seller prioritizes the buyer's needs ahead of their own. Inbound salespeople focus on the buyer's problem and context above all else. The inbound salesperson customizes their sales process and solution, should one exist. Smart leaders will take the time to learn about it, teach your sales reps how to become inbound sellers, and start using this method as a competitive advantage for your company in the age of the empowered buyer.[2]*

Sales leaders should consider an inbound selling approach if they have these problems:

- ◆ They lack a defined sales process that is routinely followed, measured, and improved.
- ◆ Executives can't determine if leads are being followed up appropriately and think opportunities may be slipping through the cracks.
- ◆ Salespeople have a hard time connecting with targeted prospects.

♦ Sales leadership needs to get more opportunities in the pipeline.

♦ The sales team spends a lot of time on low-value activities like individual one-off emails, meaningless sales calls, and leaving voice messages that are never returned.

Developing an Inbound Sales Process

To build an inbound sales process, start with evaluating your current sales model. Do your salespeople connect face-to-face or over the phone? How often do they visit customers face-to-face? Can you automate more of the connection and discovery process? Does your sales organization carry a quota? What is the percentage of salespeople hitting the quota? Do you have salespeople in the group that routinely miss quota and may not be a good fit with your organization? Do your salespeople focus on a vertical market or geographic territory? Does your sales team have enough leads or do they need more?

Once you review the organizational structure, assess individual sales productivity. How much time does a salesperson spend on customer-facing functions versus low-value administrative work? Do they have access to the tools that they need to be effective, like an easy-to-use CRM and the ability to send personalized emails? Do they have the ability to source information about good fit prospects? Do they understand the ideal buyer profile that indicates a right fit customer that provides the best long-term value for the company? Do they know the ideal buyer personas? Do they understand the emotional reasons that prospects are interested in solving the problem?

The more information available describing the ideal buyer profile, the more effective salespeople can be. An example of an ideal buyer profile is a large enterprise software company headquartered in Chicago with over 2,000 employees, six international sales offices, and more than 20 training locations selling restaurant inventory management software to regional restaurant chains.

An example of the ideal buyer persona would be the IT director, located in Dublin, responsible for collaboration at all offices, 35 years old, in her first management job, and who makes vendor selections for improving team and customer communications and collaboration.

The ideal buyer profile answers questions like:

- Is the company primarily B2B or B2C?
- What industries get the most value from solving this problem?
- Does one size of company need our help more than another?
- What defines size? Employees, locations, revenue?
- Does it matter where they are located?
- Do they use a particular technology, product, or service relating to what you offer?
- What other characteristics make them the customer?

Modern salespeople still engage with other influencers within an ideal buyer profile that do not fit the exact buyer persona, because influencers may be doing preliminary research or the decision is competitive with an established vendor.

An inbound salesperson creates a strategic process to reach, connect, discover, and understand where a buyer is in the process, their previous experience, and the help they need to make the right decision. Knowledge of the buyer profile makes it easy to create a compelling and engaging buyer experience. Inbound salespeople engage good fit prospects, understand the buyer's industry-specific vocabulary, recognize your value proposition, and have a greater appreciation for your expertise.

An inbound salesperson tries to make a psychological connection with the buyer, understanding the underlying

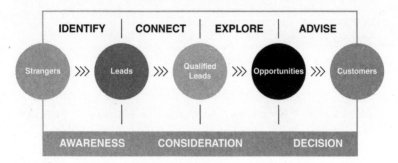

Figure 20.1   Inbound Sales Process Stages.

reasons why a prospect needs to move forward and solve a problem.

A typical inbound sales process consists of four stages:

1. Identify
2. Connect
3. Explore
4. Advise (including negotiation and closing)

These stages match up directly with the inbound buyer's journey. Identify, Connect, Explore, and Advise each describe the types of activities that happen in the stages that ultimately lead to a buying decision (see Figure 20.1).

IDENTIFY

In the Identify stage, inbound salespeople use technology and automation to identify good fit companies that correspond to the ideal buyer profile. Even if salespeople have a defined territory, they need to identify the best fit prospects in this stage. Modern buyers want to work with sellers who know their business, have relevant references, and are familiar with common buyer problems. Good fit companies that are not active in the sales process can be nurtured by marketing via account-based marketing.

The Identify stage is a shared responsibility between marketing and sales.

CONNECT

As good fit prospects become more active in pursuing a solution, they are ready to connect with your sales organization. Inbound sales people use lead notification and lead intelligence to professionally connect with good fit companies.

Traditional salespeople cold call or send undifferentiated emails to all leads with the same message and pace regardless of the fit or the persona. Inbound salespeople start out with research on the company and contact. They create a sequence of emails and phone calls that offer multiple connections over a week to 10 days. They personalize the correspondence to provide value in the first interaction. They create helpful messages that show that they are familiar with the company and connect with the contact and offer to help. If the contact isn't interested in connecting, that is OK.

The Connect stage is about improving awareness, showing expertise, offering help and guidance, and letting the buyer determine if they are ready to go to the next stage.

EXPLORE

Led by the salesperson, the Explore stage of the inbound sales process consists of a Discovery meeting to dig in deeper about the problem, its severity, and the solution required to fix the problem. Asking appropriate questions, an inbound salesperson should identify goals, plans, and challenges; define the severity of the pain; review previous attempts to solve the problem; evaluate a reasonable return on investment; understand purchase criteria; and determine the budget and purchasing process.

Rather than show up and give a product demo, an inbound salesperson asks a series of questions to determine the experience, expectations, and timeline of the prospect. This is the stage when the salesperson develops an in-depth understanding of the buyer's issues, offers assistance, and makes sure the solution can solve the buyer's problem. It's less about the product features and more about the process of learning, evaluating, and deciding to proceed to jointly solve the problem.

ADVISE

Inbound salespeople today are like consultants, offering helpful information and recommendations customized to the buyer's situation. In the Advise stage, the salesperson presents a plan that shows that they understand the fundamental problem, reviews previously stated goals to determine any changes, explains the installation and deployment of the product, points out potential roadblocks, and defines the regularity of follow up. Inbound sales connects all the dots from the buyer's perspective.

The Advise stage is where the buyer has to make three decisions.

1. Do I have everything I need to solve this problem?
2. If I move forward, what solutions should I consider?
3. Who will I work with if I decide to change and adopt a new approach?

The Advise stage also includes price negotiation and contract review, which should be conducted consistent with inbound beliefs including transparency, People First, and adding value before extracting value.

Personalize the Entire Sales Experience

Inbound sales focuses on the buyer's context and personalizing the entire sales experience. Salespeople must add value beyond what people find online, demonstrating an understanding of the company, use case, and solution.

In many cases, inbound salespeople are in a much better position to determine if they can help the buyer than a buyer is themselves. An inbound salesperson leads by asking the right questions, listens carefully, and offers to advise. It should become clear that an inbound salesperson has valuable experience to provide.

Inbound salespeople should be industry experts; they should be familiar with the pertinent content, case studies, e-books, and videos. They should leverage this experience to help buyers in similar stages by leading prospects to the appropriate strategic content. Inbound sales is built on honesty and transparency, acting like consultants with a vested interest in developing a long-term customer relationship rather than closing a deal.

Compared to traditional sales, inbound sales leads to a higher volume and velocity of qualified leads, more conversions to sales-qualified opportunities, better-fit customers, increased win rates, more net new customers, and higher revenue.

To Do

☐ Define, document, and distribute the ideal buyer profile to the sales team.

☐ Build a sales process that matches the buyer journey. Sales teams should focus on active buyers.

☐ Make sure your sales team has a modern CRM that tracks lead intelligence and lead notification without requiring manual entry.

☐ Identify two to three salespeople who can test the inbound sales process.

☐ Introduce the sales team to the inbound sales certification.

Chapter 21

Yokel Local's Strange Trip to Becoming a HubSpot Agency Partner

D arrell was mad!

"How could HubSpot say we were not a good fit for their partner program?" Darrell fumed.

Stormie Andrews and Darrell Evans started Yokel Local in Las Vegas as a local search services firm to help companies implement a digital strategy. By 2013 Yokel Local had become experts at driving web traffic for their clients, but they wanted to expand their client relationships into other services and become more of a full-service marketing firm. Both Stormie and Darrell had sales experience and wanted to build an agency that directly impacted the top line for their clients by helping them generate net new customers.

"We knew there was more to the story for our clients. They needed full marketing and sales funnel support, so we started looking for the best tools and a partner program that could help us. That is when we came to HubSpot,"[1] says Stormie.

David Weinhaus, the HubSpot partner sales rep assigned to Yokel Local, describes their first few calls this way: "They were offering their clients a local SEO type service in the Las Vegas area, so my initial thought was that these guys were not a good fit for our business. I wasn't completely sure, so I took the first call with them to ask some additional questions. Once we started talking, the differences became a bit clearer between the way they thought about the problems they solved for their clients and how HubSpot approached the problem."[2]

So, David told them, "We can't help you right now. HubSpot is not a great fit for your business."

A prospect proactively engaged with a software company with a strong intention to explore a purchase and become a certified partner and the software company said no. HubSpot didn't exactly say no, but they did say there didn't appear to be good alignment based on the information that Yokel Local provided at this time. HubSpot said, "Not now." HubSpot was following their good fit persona research. The best partner persona at the time didn't include local SEO firms but focused on agencies that covered a large regional or national footprint.

David felt that the best way that he could help Yokel Local was to use his background and experience to dig in deeper into their goals, plans, challenges, and timeline and make an honest recommendation to delay a purchase until there was more of a fit with the types of agencies that generated the best results.

David's thinking embodies the inbound sales philosophy. "I believe inbound sales is about treating prospects like I would treat my best friend. I tell them the truth even if it is not what they want to hear. My goal is to give prospects the best advice I can give them even if it means that I lose a sale, like in the case of Yokel Local."[3]

David didn't do this solely from an altruistic perspective. He explains:

> *Being selective in who we bring on as a partner makes a lot of sense for everyone involved. Based on our extensive partner experience and data, we know that a local SEO*

> *firm would be frustrated and disappointed with HubSpot if we selfishly brought them on at that point, just to close a deal. We always try to think about the long-term success of our partner relationships. If our mutual goals are incompatible, then it is always better to walk away and leave the relationship in a good place rather than take them on and create a negative experience for them and HubSpot.*[4]

Many salespeople and business owners have a tough time connecting the dots between helping first and hitting their quota or sales goals. "Helping sounds nice, but if they don't buy, it won't pay the bills—that is the fear-based excuse for selling at all costs,"[5] according to David.

So, what did Yokel Local do?

Darrell describes it this way:

> *We decided we would build our own solution—who needs those HubSpot folks anyway! We started building our inbound marketing solution by cobbling together all the tools HubSpot offered: site hosting, e-mail, SEO, blogging, and keyword tracking. We were so proud! We got these tools working for about half the cost of a HubSpot subscription, but it soon became a complete disaster. None of the technology was integrated, the separate products didn't connect to each other, and if a client left us, it was difficult to give them back their data and marketing copy.*[6]

At about that time, a new HubSpot account manager assigned to Yokel Local reached back out to Stormie and mentioned that he saw them moving into a more regional focus and expanding their concept of marketing services. And thus begins Yokel Local's official partnership with HubSpot—not when they were originally ready to buy, but when the prospect aligned with the right buyer persona.

But that is not the end of the story.

In 2015, at the annual Inbound Conference in Boston, a HubSpot employee approached David and said someone was looking for him.

It turned out that Darrell and Stormie wanted to track David down. They were now HubSpot partners and enjoying great success.

David says, "When I finally met them, they had these huge grins on their faces."[7]

The first thing Darrell said was, "You said we weren't going to be HubSpot partners two and a half years ago and now here we are. But, we have to admit, you were right. We weren't ready then and would have wasted a lot of time and money if we had moved ahead with HubSpot at that time. We had to build our agency and grow into larger projects with more national reach before we became a good fit and saw the benefits of working with HubSpot."[8]

Stormie adds, "We were very frustrated at the time, but David was 100% percent correct. When David told us no, we were very surprised. But from where we sit today the moral of the story is be honest and transparent. Stick to your ideal persona and the result will be better for everyone. You build lots of trust and credibility, and HubSpot ended up getting a better partner that will be more successful because both our goals are aligned. HubSpot helped us grow our reach and in turn, helped our clients reach their goals."[9]

What would have happened if David had sold Yokel Local when they first connected? David says: "There was a risk that they would have had a terrible experience if I either oversold them or if they had the wrong expectations. They would have recognized that they were in a tough situation and they would have had a bad taste in their mouth."[10]

This story touches on many of the critical features of an inbound organization:

♦ Work with the right buyers, not every potential buyer.
♦ Build trust by helping first and then ask them to buy.

- Put people first, over the short-term bias of closing the sale.
- Match behavior to beliefs.
- Good salespeople must adopt the inbound mindset.
- Build win-win relationships with partners.

David Weinhaus is an inbound salesperson.

Chapter 22

SMarketing

SMarketing is the process of aligning marketing and sales to work toward a common goal, drive revenue growth, and better serve prospects by enhancing the buyer's journey from first touch to customer decision. SMarketing alignment creates a seamless customer experience that echoes the values of an inbound organization.

Sales tends to focus on the 3% of buyers ready to buy now.[1] Marketing tends to focus on top-of-the-funnel metrics like impressions, visits, and total leads. SMarketing, however, focuses on building a team that addresses the concerns of buyers from the first touch through the life of the relationship.

Aligning sales and marketing teams is not simplistic. Most marketing executives get excited about the opportunity to work with their sales counterparts because it gives them more visibility, more influence, and a direct connection to revenue. It is usually the sales team that needs support and encouragement to move in this direction.

SMarketing is the best way to respond to the changes in buyer behavior defined in the first chapters of this book. Because buyers are spending more time researching online before they engage with a salesperson, lead nurturing becomes a more important component of the entire sales process. Organizations that implement SMarketing have a 20% increase in revenue. Those that don't see an average 4% decline in revenue.[2]

SMarketing makes it easy for sales because they connect to more qualified opportunities with a deep understanding of who they are talking with and ultimately close more deals. SMarketing creates better lead intelligence about the prospect and whether they fit into the ideal company profile.

SMarketing teams require a unified view of the customer to deliver value throughout the buyer journey.

Organizations practicing SMarketing provide sales with detailed individual contact lead intelligence. Examples include how many times the contact has been to the website, what content they looked at, emails they have opened, and links they have clicked through. It also includes lead notification emails or texts for these buyer behaviors as well as when someone is active on the website. SMarketing provides better lead intelligence through the entire buyer journey because this unified team views all points of the process from the first touch through the life of the relationship. The buyer journey is not separated into a marketing part and a sales part. It is viewed as one unified whole.

SMarketing provides a lead scoring mechanism that makes it easy for salespeople to spend more time with high-value prospects, rather than having to make their own decision about contact priority. SMarketing helps salespeople update current proposal templates, suggest the best content to deliver at the right stage, and automate low-value tasks.

SMarketing makes it easy for marketing teams as well because they can be sure the prospects are treated appropriately through the entire buying process. SMarketing teams have better access to data about engagement and follow up with high-quality leads. SMarketing requires the development of common goals, which ensures that high-quality leads are tracked down with multiple attempts, so good leads aren't wasted.

SMarketing teams generate better content by working together to create top-of-the-funnel content offers. Salespeople answer prospect and customer questions all day long. These answers are the best, most attractive content for inbound marketing initiatives. By publishing answers to common sales questions, the SMarketing team generates more interest around the topics that prospects care about. SMarketing makes it easy for marketing because they get a better understanding of what content works at each stage of the sales funnel.

SMarketing is essential if you want to be an inbound organization. You can't transform into an inbound organization without the alignment of these departments. If you educate and nurture prospects through the beginning phase of the buyer journey, but the sales team engages with traditional sales tactics, any trust that has been built through the process will be impacted.

Brian Signorelli, HubSpot director of the Global Sales Partner Program, says this about SMarketing:

> *After decades of discord, why would any leader care more about aligning their sales and marketing teams than in the past? One fundamental reason is that buyers have changed their behavior in such a way that requires tighter alignment between sales and marketing than ever before. Buyers, your potential customers, are delaying engaging with sales reps while consuming more and more content. So, if marketing isn't producing the right content at the right time, or the sales team doesn't know which content to share at the right time (with the right people), your company is not only going to be completely irrelevant to buyers, but it will experience eroding sales over time.*[3]

The sales team still has a profound impact on every deal. But if a prospect is doing 60 to 80% of their research online, then a modern salesperson needs to approach this prospect with the right attitude and a consistent process that reflects the philosophy of helping people first. Using traditional sales tactics on an inbound lead annoys people. Have you ever downloaded an e-book, and someone calls you two minutes later, without any research or context, and tries to push you to a demo?

Traditional organizations give an annual quota to the sales team. Inbound organizations create a shared revenue goal between marketing and sales, tie marketing to a revenue forecast, and make marketing it an investment rather than an expense.

Implementing SMarketing

There are three key steps to creating a SMarketing department:

1. Develop a common vocabulary.
2. Set common goals.
3. Create a service level agreement (SLA).

Developing a common vocabulary between marketing and sales starts with everyone agreeing on the ideal buyer persona and buyer journey. SMarketing requires agreement on definitions for leads, deal stages, and team actions. Other areas of common vocabulary include defining lead quality, handoffs between marketing and sales, lifecycle stages, and responsibilities for taking action steps.

If you ask your marketing and sales people to define a lead, will you get a consistent response? Is there agreement on a common definition?

SMarketing teams define lead stages and specify when a contact enters a particular stage. For example, when a buyer is ready to move from the Awareness to the Consideration stage, there is a point where they desire to become more engaged and talk to a salesperson. How do you define this transition point? Do marketing and sales even agree on what this point is?

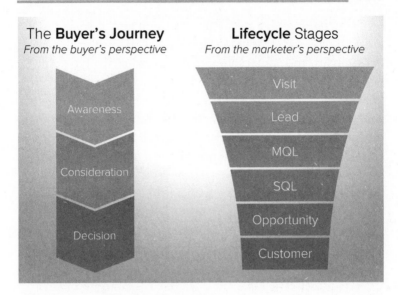

The Buyer's Journey
From the buyer's perspective

- Awareness
- Consideration
- Decision

Lifecycle Stages
From the marketer's perspective

- Visit
- Lead
- MQL
- SQL
- Opportunity
- Customer

FIGURE 22.1 Matching the Buyer Journey with Marketing and Sales Stages. *Source:* Courtesy of Hubspot.

SMarketing teams recognize this point and agree on the hand-off process (see Figure 22.1).

Common lead stages include an MQL (marketing qualified lead), a contact at a company who has filled out a form on a landing page or started a trial, and an SQL (sales qualified lead), a contact who has requested a salesperson to call them.

Set Common Goals with a Service Level Agreement

The next step in developing SMarketing alignment is to create shared goals with a service level agreement (SLA), which is used to ensure that marketing and sales teams are accountable to each other. An SLA details the specific commitments from both teams, including the goals they need to meet and the activities they will perform. Setting definitions is the foundation for creating common goals and an SLA.

A marketing SLA will define the number of leads, MQLs, and SQLs for each month. A sales SLA will define the number of calls, emails, and contact attempts for each lead by type. An SLA consists of numerical goals that lead up to the overall revenue goal. SLAs have proven to be an effective tool, with a recent study finding that 81% of companies with this type of agreement have an effective marketing strategy.[4]

When building a SMarketing SLA, each team is responsible for certain information.

Marketers should know details like:

♦ Best lead sources for highly rated leads
♦ Search, website, email, and social media conversion rate from visit to lead
♦ Number of leads each sales rep needs to hit quota
♦ Average lead-to-customer conversion percentage

Sales should know these details:

♦ How many leads a sales rep can handle
♦ How many leads sales will create on their own
♦ How many contact attempts they should make for each lead type and at what pace
♦ Average days to close by lead type

A SMarketing team needs to answer the following questions together:

♦ Who is the ideal buyer persona?
♦ What are the characteristics of the ideal buyer profile company?
♦ How are the buyer stages matched to the sales process?
♦ What is the total shared revenue goal?
♦ What are the individual sales rep quotas?
♦ What is the pace of sales attempts by lead type?

♦ Which dashboards will be used to show progress to goal?
♦ What is the average sales deal size?
♦ What is the average lead-to-customer close percentage?

SMarketing SLAs force both teams to commit to a revenue number and timeframe for completion. An SLA reflects the commitment to achieving the organizational targets as documented in the MSPOT and binds all marketing and salespeople to the same goals.

Without SMarketing, there is a high potential for misaligned goals. For example, if marketing has a goal of getting prospects to fill out a form requesting a sales meeting, but sales has a separate goal of actually scheduling those meetings, the two are not on the same page. Although the goals are similar, they are not aligned because sales must now reach out to the prospect to arrange the meeting. These added steps introduce friction into the process and result in fewer actual booked meetings.

In this example, a SMarketing team makes marketing's goal the same as the sales goal, a booked meeting. Marketing then adds a self-service scheduling option on the website conversion page for the prospect to choose a specific time for the meeting when the sales rep is available. This eliminates the disconnect, it aligns the two goals, and ends up being a better experience for the prospect.

Marketing and sales leaders set up regular reporting for the teams to review the results of the SMarketing efforts. The resulting data should be publicly shared via dashboards and reviewed regularly for accountability and early warnings of areas that require attention.

Inbound leaders create a SMarketing department by developing an agreed-upon vocabulary and setting common goals. Not only will the buyers you connect with appreciate the effort, but so will your bottom line.

To Do

- ☐ Understand the ramifications of SMarketing collaboration versus marketing and sales independence.
- ☐ Outline SMarketing collaboration in your organization today.
- ☐ Sales and marketing agree on the ideal buyer persona and buying journey.
- ☐ Define appropriate lead stages.
- ☐ Build a joint marketing and sales SMarketing service level agreement (SLA).
- ☐ Meet regularly to review the SLA and results.

Chapter 23

Tube Form Solutions—Aligning the Sales Team with Buyers

Manufacturing industrial tube fabrication equipment may not feel like the best place to apply inbound principles. However, Mike Thomas and the team at Tube Form Solutions (TFS) in Elkhart, Indiana, had other ideas.

Founded in 1989, two companies merged in 2010 to create Tube Form Solutions (TFS) to compete in a crowded marketplace. TFS designs, manufactures, and distributes tube fabrication equipment. Customers include manufacturers of automotive exhausts, heavy truck fuel systems, hydraulic lines for ships and planes, and seat frames for furniture manufacturers. They also design and manufacture tooling for tube bender and tube end forming machines. They support customers through the entire tube fabrication lifecycle from installation to refurbishments.

Unfortunately, in 2014 sales were flat. The marketing and sales playbooks that had been so successful for so long weren't working as they did before.

The main problem for Tube Form Solutions was a lack of sales qualified leads. Industry trade shows generated some leads, but not enough to grow the business. TFS was relying on their outside sales team to generate and develop their leads for new business. This resulted in missed market opportunities and missed sales targets because the sales team spent a lot of time on prospecting. The company website was not generating any leads at all.

Sales results were inconsistent among their 10 sales reps. Some were successful cold-calling for new business, some were not successful, and some flat out refused to do it. Sales reps that were new to their territories and did not have a bank of contacts to fall back on tended to get off to a slow start. Reps were vying for the "good territories," and there was a lot of heated discussion on fairness and territory realignment.

TFS thought they were staying top of mind with customers. But, after completing a review of competitive sales pursuits and analyzing the results, they realized that they were losing more often than they were winning. The company did very little ongoing engagement to market to their existing customer base. Like many companies in the industrial world, TFS focused on the people that called them requesting service and support. These people represented the proverbial "squeaky wheel." TFS also did not take much time to educate customers after the initial sale.

Mike Thomas, president of TFS, followed the HubSpot marketing blog. After reading stories of manufacturing companies succeeding with inbound marketing, he decided that TFS needed to change the way they approached marketing and sales.

TFS shifted from a total reliance on a traditional outbound approach and invested in inbound sales and marketing. They adopted the HubSpot marketing platform, CRM, and sales pro product; moved resources to inside sales; and educated everyone in the sales organization about the target persona and their buyer journey.

Thomas says:

> *We reallocated resources to inbound marketing, CRM, and more inside salespeople and technical support became our focus. We did this because our buyers told us this is how they wanted us to support them. Industrial buyers don't want*

*salespeople cold-calling them and sitting in the lobby wait-
ing to see them. Our research and experience told us that our
industrial persona wants immediate and expert support
when questions arise both before they make a sale and
especially after the sale. These people run optimized production operations and cannot have machines down. Our
expertise was being wasted with sales calls that did not
add a lot of value to the buyer or TFS. What our persona
asked for was a deeper connection to our technical expertise.
By moving more resources to engineering and technical
support we were able to help our buyers the way they want to
be helped.* *

TFS identified the key attributes of their target persona by
conducting customer and prospect interviews. Their target
persona was an engineer or business leader (often with a
technical background) who had either high-value or high-
volume tube fabrication requirements. The persona could
vary from Fortune 100 manufacturers to a local custom motor-
cycle shop. A fascinating aspect of this buyer persona research
was that TFS did really well at both ends of this production
spectrum but less well in the middle. TFS's expertise, equipment,
and business approach applied well to either persona type.

TFS developed a detailed map of the buyer journey for this
ideal buyer persona. Buying capital equipment is a complex,
multistep, considered sale and the buyer journey lasts from 6 to
12 months and includes many steps.

In general, the TFS buyer journey follows these key
milestones:

- ♦ Buyer identifies a need for automation including decision
  criteria.
- ♦ Buyer identifies potential solutions and gathers information on options.
- ♦ Buyer develops preliminary outline of specifications,
  budget, and a timeline for installation.

- Buyer validates suppliers, connecting the engineering requirements and design outline to the specifications.
- Buyer runs a supplier selection process to narrow down the list of possible vendors.
- Selected vendors perform functional tests, create prototypes, and complete technical specifications.
- Buyer develops final request for proposal and submits to a small group of vendors.
- Buyer reviews proposals of the "short list" of vendors to determine the best option.
- Buyer selects vendor, including contractual agreement and start date.
- Supplier delivers, installs, trains, and measures output.
- Supplier begins to support and service of the product to ensure success.
- Supplier conducts a periodic check to ensure proper maintenance and customer satisfaction.

TFS identified another key insight about the persona and the buyer journey; buyers asked different questions if they were a first-time buyer or buying a second or third piece of equipment. They had completely different priorities and reasons to purchase. Also, buyers fell into one of two orientations. Either they were ROI focused and looking for the best price-performance ratio or they were detail/specification focused and needed a very specific feature to make the investment work.

Detail-oriented personas knew their production lines inside and out. They wanted to know the specific details of all the equipment they might add to their very controlled environment. They were very picky because they took pride in their work and felt personal ownership of the production line.

Results-oriented personas knew their business and production processes well enough, but they cared less about the actual production line and more about results. They wanted to know how tube fabrication equipment impacts and improves the production process, or increases speed, or reduces waste, or improves the bottom line.

Buyers tended to stay in the same lane, although some would go from results to detail oriented for subsequent purchases because of experience, change of ownership, or different market conditions. TFS was able to determine this buyer perspective via their marketing data and could address either option. If TFS delivers the appropriate return, then future purchases become more specification oriented, often with TFS being the only vendor considered.

Once over the specification and engineering detail hurdles, detail-oriented buyers often want to see how a new machine increases their return when they add it to their existing operation. The insight that personas may change their focus depending on the long-term stage of their journey is an important one for TFS. It helps them stay alert to the types of questions they are being asked, so they respond with the right information.

Once TFS understood and documented the persona and buyer journey information, they completed a content audit matching existing content assets to the persona and buyer journey stages.

This audit included:

- ◆ Specific checklists and guides for purchasing tooling and machines
- ◆ "Tool School" training documents designed to educate readers and help them successfully operate the equipment
- ◆ Introductory content about their equipment to help "explain to the boss" how this machine would fit into the production line and provide an effective ROI
- ◆ E-books and video presentations with technical details about the equipment, usage, and applications suitable for engineers

♦ ROI calculators that helped buyers know when automation paid off in fabricated part volume and value and how long it would take to get a reasonable ROI

TFS took these content assets and started running marketing campaigns. They built landing pages for each of the content assets like e-books and slide decks. TFS also built thank you pages that provided the content offer. These pages encouraged further engagement with the sales team to answer questions or get more detailed information. They created lead nurturing email campaigns encouraging prospects to request quotes or contact the sales team to discuss their project at any stage of the buying process. TFS figured out what parts of the website were driving the most traffic and used calls to action to point traffic from those pages to the landing pages and offers of machines that would upgrade that experience.

"Most of our content is very engineering-heavy, technical stuff that proves popular with our target audience,"* says Thomas.

Content is a big focus. Most of the content that previously existed talked about what TFS machines did and the applications they addressed. TFS organized the existing application content into a library so that they could show the full range of solutions and the benefit they created. The goal was to create strategic content to build a bigger audience. They wanted the website to be a resource destination for engineers dealing with tube fabrication issues that covers the entire lifecycle of a tube from the tube mill to the finished component.

TFS developed detailed segmentation of their contact database by persona, then created additional marketing automation workflows that nurture these segments. The goal is to deliver personal, focused messages to the right persona. These messages include case studies from existing customers, as many companies are dealing with similar issues.

TFS also implemented HubSpot CRM and trained their sales teams on how to nurture and engage with inbound leads over the phone.

What was the reaction from the sales team?

Thomas explains:

The sales team got busy fast! These changes caused some confusion within the team. Salespeople didn't know how to connect with leads who weren't yet ready to buy. New lead qualification outlines helped the sales team respond to each e-book download lead or request for quote lead. We trained them on nurturing leads who are starting their buying process. We stopped going for the sale close right off the bat when a prospect downloaded a top-of-the-funnel offer. We started to ask more questions, which helped our people understand what problem they were trying to solve, what application they needed to implement, and what results they were looking for.*

By implementing HubSpot CRM, the sales team now tracked and shared their activity with leads and deals, giving TFS better insight into their pipeline. TFS's salespeople did not use a CRM before this, even though they had one installed.

TFS leveraged HubSpot's sales technology to help them get more out of their traditional marketing and sales approaches. Trade shows are still critical in the capital equipment world, and TFS uses landing pages and offers to get booth visitors to convert back on the website once they return from the event. The sales team then engages those contacts with more personalized content to improve the relationship and boost the ROI that TFS sees from their trade show investments.

Thomas says, "Engineers use the Internet to do their research, and wait until later in their buying process to contact companies like ours. TFS did not serve early-stage prospects with our website until we adopted inbound. We feel we are getting ahead of it now. Persona-based content has made our events better and improved the types of conversations we have with the people we meet. Networking on LinkedIn is more effective using this content, which gets us in front of even more qualified buyers. People come to our booth and let us know they read an article or learned a lot from an e-book. Our sales team started to hear from the prospects that they appreciated and consumed our content, and saw the benefits of what we were doing. Our salespeople were skeptics, but they see now why an inbound strategy works."*

TFS committed to using more of the HubSpot CRM features and to taking advantage of the marketing and sales integration they provides. The HubSpot CRM collects a leads website and email history (because it shares a common database with the marketing platform), which allows the salespeople to manage the sales process. As a result, the time frame for closing deals has drastically shortened. TFS also created new dashboards and reports in the HubSpot CRM, which allowed them to track key account activity. This tracking makes it possible for them to react with the appropriate context and personal messaging when a contact needs help.

TFS started to use Google Adwords to present their content offers to more searchers on more keywords. They test and evaluate where their buyers look for information and what they are looking for. TFS moved from advertising the products to promoting their offers using Google Adwords and targeted trade media. This change to an inbound philosophy for outbound advertising increased lead generation by 200% from the same trade journal e-newsletters. This change in approach invested in these outbound types of ads ROI positive.

"Now, our challenge is to up our game and the value that our sales team brings. Over time, we will continue to transition more sales assets to the inside and technical sales roles. Our customers expect technical expertise from our sales team and applications experience from our service people so they can get the right solution recommendation. TFS has a very technical and experienced sales team, and we will continue the process of learning how to convert that knowledge to content that buyers want to consume," states Thomas.

What happened as a result of these changes?

"The number and quality of our leads increased immediately. We landed many sales and found new customers that would have never considered us if it had not been for inbound. We increased our sales over $1,000,000 in year one after adopting an inbound mindset. The results spoke for themselves and made it easy for us to continue to invest more time and resources to inbound ideas, technology, and services," says Thomas.

He continues, "We plan to create more content around tube bending tooling and consumables. We will engage more with existing customers to provide increasing value in the relationship. We will create specific content that relates to the engineering issues our customers see every day. Another area of focus is marketing our expertise to our existing customers. We will drive our inbound marketing efforts farther into the lifecycle journey and add more resources to stay engaged after the sale. We know that shipping a machine and starting it up is not enough. Our customers need to be successful with our equipment for as long as they use it, which is almost always many years and in some cases decades."

Thomas concludes by saying, "We will continue to apply the principles of inbound to everything we do. We will bring more people throughout the company into the process of being as helpful to our prospects and customers as possible. Especially after the sale when the relationship with our team and us matters the most to the buyer."*

TFS has become an inbound organization.

Chapter 24

Inbound Service

Today, your service organization is more important than your sales organization when it comes to generating net new customers. This may be somewhat controversial, but in the age of modern buyers doing their research online, examples of tangible customer success matter more than empty sales promises. Potential buyers trust current users who have gone through a recent purchasing experience more than they trust a new salesperson who has a vested interest in closing a deal. Most businesses invest in new sales talent to get net new customers. For inbound organizations, investing in a better customer experience to create a legion of loyal customers, who share their success with others, is a better investment.

Inbound service is about applying inbound principles to your service organization. It includes all the resources that support a customer after the sale, including installation technicians, onboarding consultants, technical support, trainers and education teams, and even account managers and customer success managers.

Inbound organizations define success regarding the individual buyer's goals and expectations. They identify and discuss these goals and expectations during the Consideration and Decision stages of the inbound sales process. Inbound service organizations take the hand-off from the sales team, review the pertinent information, establish control of the customer relationship, and outline a plan that delivers results to ensure ongoing customer satisfaction.

Inbound service does not wait for the phone to ring. They use a centralized view of the customer to recognize a milestone, due date, or other critical event to reduce the effort required for buyers to accomplish their goals. An inbound service organization understands that the average customer is busy, doesn't spend all their time engaged with the product, and welcomes insightful information and advice. This means responding to a problem in minutes and hours, rather than days and weeks. Inbound service respects the customer's time and doesn't keep them endlessly on hold. Modern buyers want companies to use technology solutions like chat, instant messaging, and call me now buttons that provide trained services personnel 24/7.

Inbound service is a series of activities, processes, and tasks that result in the buyer feeling like they are treated the way they want to be treated with their problem solved in the way they want it to be solved. Inbound service reduces cancellations and dissatisfaction, improves customer retention, drives vendor loyalty, and creates an opportunity to cross-sell and upsell by solving for the customer's success first.

A survey by *Harvard Business Review* found the following:

First, delighting customers doesn't build loyalty; reducing their effort—the work they must do to get their problem solved—does.

Second, acting on this insight improves customer service, reduces customer service costs, and decreases customer cancellations.[1]

The story from the survey goes further: "But our research shows that exceeding their expectations during service interactions (for example, by offering a refund, a free product, or a free service such as expedited shipping) makes customers only marginally more loyal than simply meeting their needs."

And it gets worse. The study found that "customers are four times more likely to leave a service interaction disloyal than loyal." So satisfied does not mean loyal. Typical customer service makes loyalty worse!

And if that is not enough how about this quote from a recent Accenture survey:

> *Our research revealed that consumers are increasingly likely to have a negative reaction to a company's attempt to earn their loyalty.*

And one more quote from the same survey:

> *That means calibrating investments to focus on retaining customers with highly satisfying experiences and leveraging their connections to acquire new customers. That's where the hidden pools of loyalty returns lie.*[2]

Traditional companies ask their customer service people to fix a problem, address an issue, or figure it out. They manage to response times, not to outcomes. They view the goal of customer service as fixing the customer's immediate problem while minimizing the financial impact to their company. The problem with that approach is that it rarely addresses the more critical issues facing the customer.

Defining the Customer Journey

The customer goes through a journey (similar to a buyer journey) where they transition from the purchase to product installation, to seeing the potential of the product, to starting to use the product, to solving the problem the purchase was intended to solve.

This journey is defined in four stages:

1. Activation
2. Day Zero
3. Time to Value
4. Value Loop

ACTIVATION

The Activation stage begins with the buyer's first interactions with your product or service. These may include activities like logging in to the software or account, setting up the payment method, receiving delivery of physical product, opening the box the product came in, receiving confirming emails, scheduling training, or product set up. Inbound organizations have a seamless integration from the buyer journey to the customer journey to capitalize on the initial enthusiasm of getting started and maintaining the positive experience.

Why is this handoff essential? Because in the age of the modern buyer, customers have a very low pain threshold for dealing with unanticipated problems, and the seller is responsible for creating an efficient initial startup process to make sure the customer gets off to a good start. Is there anything more discouraging to a modern buyer than deciding to purchase a product or service and then stumbling right out of the gate? Or the chilling realization that buying the product may not solve the problem you intended it to solve? Or coming to the conclusion that the organization that was helpful and attentive to your needs during the sales process is a bit less enthusiastic about helping you after you have paid the bill?

DAY ZERO

Day Zero is the second stage of the process and is "the moment when a customer has completed the necessary tasks, so they start to realize the full value of your product for the job they are hiring it to do."[3] A buyer that fails to reach this point, or takes too long to reach this stage, runs the risk of churning, burning, or indifference. The goal of Day Zero is to get everyone to the point of being able to extract value from your solution. Day Zero marks the transition from startup to usage.

Time to Value

The Time to Value stage is when the buyer is starting to be successful using the product or service. An inbound organization understands the Time to Value timeline for each category of user and prescribes a project plan that defines the optimal customer journey. This plan describes the work involved and the maintenance of the product, sets the right expectations for frequency of usage, and explains the specific details of what to do. First, the organization defines how to get help if the customer gets in a pickle, and they show the customer how to stay on track.

Time to Value is the interval it takes from Day Zero to the first time customers begin to extract value from the product or service and begin on the path of reaching their goals. For some products and services, the Time to Value stage is seconds or minutes, while others may take months or years. An app that you download to your mobile phone and start using immediately has a short Time to Value. A complex ERP system with significant layers of implementation and integration, development and end-user training, technical customization, and hundreds of rollout steps may take many years to reach the Time to Value stage.

Value Loop

The last stage in the customer journey is the Value Loop. A Value Loop starts at the point where the customer recognizes they are being successful and are open to investigating additional products and services from your organization to solve other problems. A Value Loop ends when the customer buys additional products, add-ons, or services. Inbound service creates Value

Loops when they present buyers with better solutions to new issues and the buyer accepts and implements them.

The Value Loop stage creates an excellent environment for buyers to try before they buy because of the familiarity and trust established in the customer journey. Offering options to evaluate new features, makes sense because customers have a basic understanding of the product.

Marketing to existing customers is often misunderstood. Companies pour the majority of investment into sales teams with the goal of generating net new customers. Inbound organizations know that the best way to drive revenue, at the lowest cost, is to focus on existing customers and offer opportunities to help them even more.

HubSpot's Value Loops occur when the user is leveraging the product on a daily basis. HubSpot recognizes that activity and periodically presents a special offer to the user to test an advanced software feature or application that would enhance the buyer's experience. Another example is a customer showing interest in paid advertising based on their behavior within HubSpot: the software then suggests a paid add-on application upgrade or third party integration.

How Do You Build the Ideal Customer Journey?

Start with the ideal buyer persona and work backward, understanding how your most successful customers reach their goals using your product or service. Study the actual customers and see what steps they took, assistance you provided, and roadblocks they encountered, and begin to build a detailed map of the stages in the success journey. Analyze which customers entered a Value Loop, bought again, or added to their original purchase, and where customers get hung up and just stop engaging with you.

The next part of this process is to define Day Zero. Figure out when the customer reaches the point of being able to use your solution on their own. Next, list the steps customers must go through to complete the Activation stage.

Once you complete those steps, you can map out the customer journey. Data and analytics are crucial to understanding exactly how the customer journey is laid out. There is usually a difference in retention rates or repeat sales for customers who reach Day Zero before or at the projected date versus those who take longer. Understanding why specific customers get stuck in the Activation stage should help you identify common bottlenecks and help you improve the Time to Value. If you know the expected Time to Value for your ideal buyer persona customers, you can give better guidance about success rates and activities.

What Buyers Expect from Inbound Service

Inbound organizations recognize and provide quick, efficient, proactive service to meet the modern buyer's expectations. Buyers are more impatient than ever and expect personal responses immediately. Proper planning enables speed of response and alignment between all departments. If service correctly anticipates and staffs for new clients, then they rightly plan and prevent a slow response.

For most modern buyers, self-service is excellent service. A unique way to provide information is a service knowledge base. A service knowledge base consists of a public posting of the most frequently asked questions, training videos, customer feedback, and helpful hints. Posting an open knowledge base provides several crucial advantages. First, it allows everyone to research and educate at their own pace. Second, it allows for 24/7 access. Third, building up a knowledge base of questions provides underlying data about potential potholes in the customer success journey.

Some inbound service organizations even let partners answer questions in the knowledge base for the broader community. By providing a knowledge base, you are providing more information while reducing your service costs. From travel arrangements to grocery store checkout, modern buyers expect and appreciate self-service options.

Inbound service teams have a unique perspective on the buyer journey. In the age of the modern buyer, identifying, planning, and executing an effective customer success journey significantly impacts retention and new business development, often to a greater level than efforts to add net new customers to increase revenue.

To Do

- ☐ Determine if your service team is proactive or reactive.
- ☐ Ensure that your service team can respond in minutes, not hours.
- ☐ Work backward from successful customers and map their customer journey.
- ☐ Ask your customers what they consider great service.

Chapter 25

Measuring the Health of Your Relationships

The key to leveraging inbound service as part of a new business development strategy is happy customers. Measuring the health of your relationships will help you understand which customers are thrilled, where you are exceeding expectations, which customers are in good shape, and which customers fall below the minimum threshold for success.

Service teams need to have all the customer's information for success, for example, call back information, email addresses, phone numbers, account numbers, order history, payment terms, service records of past issues and fixes, and relevant meeting notes to build the proper context for their interactions. They need a centralized view of the customer every bit as much as the marketing and sales teams.

To build a customer success mindset into your service department, inbound organizations create a separate team alongside service. HubSpot calls this group inbound success to clearly differentiate their mission. Inbound service means reacting promptly to all requests and solving the immediate issues customers have. Inbound success is the proactive application of a process to ensure customers see long-term value from your products and services and benefit from using your solutions. Inbound success focuses on making the customer better and delivering more value after the initial sale is made.

Health Check as a Best Practice

Inbound success requires that your team knows the status of every customer relationships at every point in time. You must understand the progress toward achieving the goals agreed upon when the customer bought your solution.

HubSpot starts thinking about the health of every customer in the activation stage then assesses customer health periodically through the customer journey. At least 180 days before a contract comes up for annual renewal the customer renewal team reviews all available information and runs a detailed "health check" to assess how successful each customer is with the product.

Health checks are an analysis process that determines the customer's usage of the product, results they are receiving measured against their goals, and the overall experience. Health checks are a programmatic way to conduct an in-depth investigation into the success of the customer using the products, with an emphasis on progress toward their goals.

Mike Ewing, HubSpot customer renewal manager, says:

Health checks have produced an impactful benefit to our customers' success by identifying specific areas for specialized team members to address. We look at over 20 different factors to conclude if a customer is in a Green, Yellow, Orange, or Red category. The four categories are:

1. *Overall Health*
2. *Product Usage Health*
3. *Value Health*
4. *Experience Health*

Once documented in HubSpot's CRM, we pass the health checks onto the account management team, which creates playbooks matching the results of the health check category.

These playbooks guide the team to provide content and resources the customer needs to maximize their chances of meeting their goals and renewing their HubSpot agreement. This focused assistance to our customer base has been a significant driver of increased customer happiness and success.

I love that HubSpot is constantly striving to proactively drive customer success and value. Health checks are the latest iteration, and are a process I think that can be adapted and adopted by many companies of all shapes and sizes.[1]

For HubSpot, about 80% of a health check is evaluated by reviewing the customer's usage of the product and 20% is subjective. Usage data includes login frequency, application use, emails sent, and workflow creation. The health check also considers the success customers are seeing using the products such as leads converted and customers acquired. Some of the subjective assessments include looking at the customer's website to see if they are following inbound marketing best practices, the quality of the blog posts they are publishing, and reviewing the content of emails and social media posts.

HubSpot starts the health check process six months before the renewal date so that they are proactive and address any lingering issues that can be solved. Three months after the health check-up, the customer success team reassesses the account to see if there has been measurable progress. This proactive process, starting well before the renewal date, drives the customer's success and maintains a high retention rate.

HubSpot uses the health check process to notice trends with healthy customers as well. The service team is aligned with the sales account management team and regularly shares health check feedback when they see opportunities for sales to reengage with a customer and point out a small success, explain an area of concern, or advise them even more.

Inbound success is proactive, jumping in before a customer gets stuck. Inbound success relies on a solve for the customer attitude, as much as data and process. Inbound service people must be empowered, motivated, and compensated appropriately.

Giving your service team bad tools and incomplete information, sending them a bunch of angry customers, and asking them to fix the relationship doesn't make sense in the age of buyer control.

Service Alignment with Marketing and Sales

Marketing, sales, and service form the backbone of the customer success team. Inbound organizations align all three around the same inbound strategy. Sales, marketing, and service alignment revolve around three key components:

1. Customer volume and pace
2. Good customer fit
3. Team communication

To provide adequate staffing levels, allocate resources, and define an effective service plan, an inbound service team needs to know the number and type of buyers projected to start at any given time. Seasonality throughout the year, and velocity during the month, impacts this schedule.

Two of the largest failures of traditional service departments are:

1. Inability to define the buyer success journey in a systematic and detailed way
2. Limited resources available at the day and time they are needed

Good customer fit is as important as pace and volume. The better the fit of the customer to the buyer persona, the greater the chance of buyer success after the sale.

Michael Redbord says, "The goal is to align the promise of value, made during the earlier stages of the buyer journey, with the achievement of success by the buyer once the customer success journey begins. The promise of value must align with what the inbound service and success teams manage, so the buyer's expectations are met."[2]

Marketing, sales, and service/success alignment requires constant feedback loops. The leaders of the sales and service departments must be in regular contact exchanging data and context so that both groups adjust and help each other, as needed. The most valuable asset the inbound organization has is the contact/customer database, which includes information about the buyer's behavior. The data gathered during the early buying stages should be shared with the inbound service and success teams, so they deliver on the value promises made to the buyer and meet or exceed their expectations.

In turn, inbound service and success teams feed data and context back to the sales team to improve both the individual customer relationship as well as to adjust future customer acquisition. The information gleaned from successful customers is helpful for inbound salespeople to understand so they can identify new good fit customers. A sound communication loop allows the inbound service and success teams to give the lead back to the salesperson at the appropriate time to start the Value Loop stage, thus extending the relationship with the buyer even further.

To Do

- ☐ Define a health check process.
- ☐ Identify the steps in a customer success journey.
- ☐ Implement inbound service and inbound success as unique teams.

Chapter 26

Inbound Back Office

The great irony of this information age is that, in many ways, we actually know less about the sources of value in the economy than we did fifty years ago. In fact, much of the change has been invisible for a long time simply because we did not know what to look for. There's a huge layer of the economy unseen in the official data and, for that matter, unaccounted for on the income statements and balance sheets of most companies.
— Erik Brynjolfsson and Andrew McAfee[1]

The back office, typically defined as the non-customer-facing departments that manage business operations, is rarely thought of as being responsible for customer success. But in the new age of buyer control, all employees should be familiar with the ideal customer profile, understand the buyer personas, and be aware of their impact on the buyer journey.

The inbound back office creates enterprise value by helping to improve the buyer's journey and adding value to the customer success journey.

The back-office business operation departments typically include finance, accounting, IT, and legal. An inbound organization runs business operations with the same values as the front-office departments: putting people first, emphasizing the culture, recruiting effectively for employees with the right values, and reinforcing the mission, vision, strategies, and plays. Back-office employees should go through the same onboarding experience as sales, marketing, and services employees.

Do Finance and Accounting Help Your Customer's Experience?

In the traditional business model, finance and accounting are administrative functions responsible for producing accurate financial documentation that analyzes past performance, identifies potential financial issues, and helps leaders avoid or mitigate risks in the future. Most of the emphasis is on reporting and control, compliance, and fiscal management. These are all necessary business functions essential to successful operation. Most business leaders don't consider these back-office functions when they think about creating superior customer experiences and building better customer relationships.

Inbound organizations ask billing, accounting, and finance to solve for the customer and assist in the buyer and customer success journey. In addition to the basic administrative functions, the back office provides a deep level of decision support for customer-facing teams. Finance and accounting must help the company surface the value that is invisible to standard financial practices, value that is a critical component of an inbound organization's strategy and success.

Customer interaction with finance and accounting is rare, but these episodes can make or break relationships. Have you ever had a positive interaction with a financial or accounting department? One where they knew your name, recognized your status, had easy access to your customer records, listened to your inquiry, and settled the issue with one email or phone call? You felt special, empowered, and happy.

Now consider how many negative experiences you have had in the last year paying bills, stopping a service, reversing a charge, or disputing an entry. Some companies make it hard to pay a bill, or they supply confusing, conflicting, or misleading billing statements. Some companies surprise you with unauthorized charges. Some companies provide email as the only recourse for resolving an issue. A customer interaction with billing or finance is often the least considered step in the process, from the seller's point of view, but is critically important in the customer success journey.

Traditional finance departments focus on processing a transaction rather than helping the customer navigate the buying process in a way that adds to the customer experience. Inbound organizations make the finance department accountable for the customer success journey. Does your billing or accounting department ever consider the customer experience in their day-to-day activities?

Accounting, billing, and legal teams are in a tough spot. If they are too rigid and internally focused, they can make good customers immediately regret their purchasing decision. Have you ever had seven pages of 8-point-type terms and conditions text jammed down your throat right at the point of purchase? Inbound billing, accounting, and legal departments are very aware of the impact that they have on customer satisfaction and experience and recognize the impact they have from the customer's perspective.

A few years ago, as HubSpot was growing quickly, they realized they were losing customers at the first annual contract renewal. Because some customers received a promotional offer or discount for the first year of using the HubSpot platform, the yearly renewal at full price came as a bit of a surprise. This was not a good way to introduce the fact that the price was going up to standard levels. Customers perceived it as an immediate price increase.

HubSpot decided to implement a contract renewal process led by a dedicated customer renewal success team. This team holed up at HubSpot offices in Cambridge, Massachusetts, for over a month to study the data, review customer behavior, and model a better process. The team invested time in understanding the ideal buyer persona at the renewal stage of the customer success journey, and to examine how customers want to be treated and served at this critical point in the relationship.

The customer renewal team worked with the finance team to develop a renewal model where customers would be able to choose their price. HubSpot didn't want to have conversations with loyal customers and haggle over a new discount for extending a subscription. The team came up with a self-service option that provided the customer the renewal process they wanted.

HubSpot would sometimes exchange a longer contract period from the customer in return for discounted fees. Customers could essentially pick their pricing. The lower the price, the longer the commitment that was required. This resulted in a classic win-win between HubSpot and the customer.

Mike Ewing, HubSpot customer renewal manager, says:

> *Raising prices after extending a discount to get the relationship started makes sense in a competitive environment. But when it comes time for renewal, we can't say, "Here's your bill. Pay it." That sets us up for confrontation and a negative customer experience. By conducting health checks, starting the renewal process well before the contract due date, and allowing customers to pick their ongoing price, we build on our relationship and let our customers get even more value from HubSpot when we have renewal discussions. Our finance team gave us the tools to be able to have the renewal conversations in the right context and tone, one of helpfulness and partnership.*[2]

Most finance and accounting departments are not connected to the customer acquisition and relationship building process like this. They are unaware and unconcerned about their impact on the customer experience. They are set up to efficiently process orders regardless of the impact on the customer success journey.

An inbound organization leverages billing, accounting, and finance as an opportunity to enhance the customer success journey.

Finance's Role Moving Forward

Inbound organizations embrace the role of the finance, billing, and accounting departments in the customer success journey. They create positive customer experiences by designing effective payment terms, transaction and billing methods, and financing options designed to make it easy for prospects to buy. They design the details of the financial process with the input of marketing, sales, and service teams and then they make sure that the processes are successful via quick surveys and customer check-ins. Inbound finance teams work with marketing, sales, and service to develop the right metrics and key performance indicators to measure and then report regularly on their progress.

An inbound finance team should create models and profiles for identifying good fit customers regarding the cost of customer acquisition, lifetime value of a customer, annual contract value, monthly recurring revenue, gross margin percent, support costs, customer churn, and other critical finance milestones in the customer success journey.

Inbound finance leaders understand that responsiveness and follow-through is crucial, and that modern buyers expect help along the way. Financial interactions that remain honest, engaging, and buyer focused help retain good fit customers.

Inbound Value on the Balance Sheet

Todd tells this story of inbound value:

> *A client once asked us to help grow the value of their business because he wanted either to sell it or pass it along to his son.*

They chose an inbound strategy to grow awareness, drive targeted leads, and expand into a new market. The company was a regional manufacturer located in Texas, in the oil and gas industry. Over a four-year period, we helped them grow the business while expanding into new geographies because the improved performance of the website allowed them to connect with potential dealers around the world.

When the business eventually sold, we asked the owner how his company was valued by the acquiring firm.

His answer was "Three."

I said, "Three? Three what?"

He replied, "Three times what the company was worth before we started implementing inbound."

Breaking down the cost justification of the purchase was fascinating. The acquiring company used a standard valuation approach to measure the revenue and cash flow increases resulting from more leads and sales. They also placed a premium value on the global brand recognition and a series of marketing assets that didn't exist before the move to inbound. They put a premium valuation on these inbound assets, like high-ranking organic keywords and the expanded contact list, including detailed lead intelligence about each contact and their engagement activity. They put an additional value on the process for communicating with and converting contacts from casual prospects into active buyers.

The buyer was willing to pay a premium for the company because they were an inbound organization. This inbound equity was a direct result of inbound activities, processes, and resources that built the value of the organization.

In this case, inbound assets valued by the acquiring company justified a premium price.

A company in our industry went out of business. The creditors held an auction to sell off the assets. There were millions of dollars' worth of capital equipment for sale, along with the standard office equipment like desks, chairs, and telephones. The company failed due to a combination of unethical business practices and poor customer retention, but they did a good job with content creation and SEO. When the company assets went to auction, everything sold for pennies on the dollar, except for one item. Their central web server.

This server held all the website assets, all site content, and contact data from the company CRM. The server was the most sought-after item for sale because of the inbound assets that it contained. The educational content, inbound links, landing pages, calls to action, and the inherent keyword ranking was way more valuable to the buyers than any other physical asset. The book value of the server was a few thousand dollars; the assets contained on the server sold for more than $500,000 at auction.

Inbound Legal

A legal department can contribute to building enterprise value while solving for the customer as part of an inbound back office.

Radical transparency, an essential part of an inbound culture, works the same way with legal terms and conditions. Transparency applied to the customer success journey means clearly stating legal information on your website for everyone to view. This includes information like data usage parameters, privacy policies, definitive terms of use, and conditions of service. Inbound legal teams have to maintain a delicate balance: they have to protect the legitimate interests of the organization while protecting the rights of their customer without impacting the buyer experience. Inbound legal teams find the balance between transparency, liability, and regulatory compliance.

John Kelleher, HubSpot chief legal counsel, describes his team this way: "We are looking at ways to stay ahead of the curve and provide conscious customer engagement at points in the journey like payment and renewals. The key is to develop trust in the relationship."[3]

Most modern buyers don't consider terms and conditions an important component of a great customer experience, but inbound legal departments make sure the information is accessible on the website, available in multiple languages, and states points clearly.

Buying HubSpot software is pretty simple from a final transaction perspective. The buyer completes a short form, enters their credit card number, and hits the complete the transaction button. But what if you are in Japan and the only binding legal terms are written in English and must be approved in English?

At the point of completing the transaction, a buyer is faced with the prospect of reading 18 pages of legal jargon that may or may not be understandable to the buyer. Throw in the possibility that you are not a native English speaker, and you now have a touch point in the process that is less than helpful from the buyer's perspective.

Frank Auger, HubSpot CIO, explains HubSpot's response:

We translated the terms and conditions into Japanese, and some other languages, even though the buyer must agree to the terms in English. At least now they can see in their native language and understand what it is they agree to. We will continue to build more and more transparency into the legal details of the process, so we do not detract from the experience of our buyers at the point they are deciding to finalize the agreement and move ahead with HubSpot.[4]

During the transactional steps in customer onboarding, HubSpot creates a very user-friendly terms of service document and outlines the details for each buyer. The nonlegalese content is designed to provide a quick reference point, educate new users on the basics, and state the commitments from both parties.

With these steps, the HubSpot legal team meets the velocity of the buyer journey and does not slow it down. This education process solves for customers first, reduces customer churn, and eliminates many potential issues for the sales and service teams down the road.

John Kelleher further states:

> *We see legal as being a supporter of the inbound culture by helping employees prepare for and manage the responsibilities of transparency. Transparency also imposes a burden on legal. We cannot only say no but must explain our decisions regarding the culture code and the business objectives. We must be transparent with our team, including partners and vendors because we know this process builds trust.*[5]

An inbound legal team routinely works with customer-facing teams and trains them on legal issues like terms and conditions and cancellation policies. The principles of inbound apply to the legal department as well. Legal should train, educate, and share content with employees about the legal policies and decisions that impact them and their ability to deliver an inbound customer experience.

Inbound IT

Inbound organizations run on data. An inbound IT department provides the core systems and data to make decisions closest to the customer. Inbound IT teams provide the tools that allow your business to get that data, organize it, and share it. The organization then develops insights and actions improving the customer experience, using a centralized view of the customer. An inbound IT organization supports a People First inbound culture, creates a departmental MSPOT, and is in alignment with the mission of the company.

An inbound IT team is focused on building the infrastructure needed to support the customer success journey. This process includes a modern CRM, marketing automation system, and the office automation applications to fill in the gaps. IT must stop turning their backs on customers to protect the walls they have built around their department. We have seen too many examples of IT people putting self and department over the best interests of the company and the best interests of their customers.

We know of numerous examples of IT departments hobbling marketing and sales teams with obsolete systems for managing websites, tracking customer data, and communicating with customers. In the name of protecting their turf, IT prevents the organization from adapting to the changes in buyer behavior.

IT should develop the inbound customer technology stack and collaborate with the customer team to create digital insights for leaders to track the buyer journey and monitor the customer experience. The technical tools exist to do this. What is lacking is the vision, motivation, and accountability for IT to make it happen. Connecting IT to the culture and using tools like an MSPOT will align IT with the mission of the company.

IT is important in the transition to inbound because they can be either a huge bottleneck or a huge benefit. Transparency, autonomy, frequent communication, using data to make decisions closest to the customer, and building trust all require technology to master. Becoming an inbound organization requires IT to lead the charge to facilitate communication internally and externally using appropriate tools.

Bringing the inbound organization and inbound beliefs to the back office will be the true test of whether leaders completely buy into these ideas.

To Do

☐ Create finance, accounting, legal, and IT departmental MSPOTs.

☐ Review/audit current practices and identify gaps and opportunities for alignment with an inbound culture.

☐ Begin training these departments in inbound methodology, culture, and practices.

Chapter 27

Inbound Ecosystems

An inbound ecosystem is a local, regional, or possibly global community that organizations join or create, with shared interests and a shared philosophy. The ecosystem evolves to solve common problems or address common issues with all participants adding their area of expertise. One or more companies establish leadership of the ecosystem and help the members align with a shared vision. Resources and investments follow the shared vision.

Inbound ecosystems are made up of a variety of different constituents with different roles that believe in win-win relationships between all parties.

Inbound ecosystems include:

- Employees and contractors
- Investors and stockholders
- Prospects (including lurkers, content consumers, and potential buyers)
- Customers
- Suppliers of complementary products or third-party applications
- Partners, including distribution channels and service partners
- Industry groups, trade associations, government bodies
- Competitors

Software platforms like HubSpot intentionally create an ecosystem to better support clients. HubSpot partners are part of this ecosystem because they sell to and support customers and users and help them get better results. Third-party application developers are part of the ecosystem because they create apps that link into the core platform. Integration software and services companies are welcomed into the ecosystem to help develop connections into HubSpot that extend the features and power of the software into more areas. Partners, customers, and prospects attend HubSpot user groups to educate and support each other, teach best practices, improve community knowledge, and learn from each other.

HubSpot also created an event called INBOUND. It's a week-long celebration that welcomes tens of thousands of people to Boston every year as a way to raise awareness, build industry acceptance of the inbound philosophy, and create a place for like-minded people to connect with each other and learn more.

HubSpot has created online communities as well. Inbound .org is a community of over 145,000 members sharing ideas, concepts, opinions, announcements, open job positions, available talent, and assistance in vetting local resources. The HubSpot Academy is a complete online training community, built to provide documentation, training, guides, podcasts, and videos to teach primary, intermediate, and advanced inbound subjects. The HubSpot Academy offers 16 different certifications at no charge to anyone who would like to improve their inbound knowledge. There are hundreds of topics relating to inbound covered somewhere in the Academy. HubSpot provides this fantastic resource to everyone, including competitors and buyers who use competitive products, because HubSpot believes in helping everyone first. A first-time visitor to the HubSpot Academy home page will be offered a simple question above a search box: "What do you want to learn today?" The rest is up to them, but the offer to help, educate, inform, and advise stands open and free to anyone who asks, with no expectation of payment to HubSpot.

Not only that, but if you take an online class in the Academy, HubSpot provides you with free software to try to help you even more.

The HubSpot Academy is a strong example of an inbound ecosystem that consistently provides value.

The Ideas behind an Inbound Ecosystem

Two ideas underline the importance of the inbound ecosystem concept. First, any one individual is no more than six people away from any other person in the world (more commonly known as the six degrees of Kevin Bacon). This theory suggests that everyone on earth is no more than six acquaintances away from any other person on the planet. Digital disruption creates a world in which everyone connects. It is your choice if you choose to acknowledge it, participate in it, and take advantage of it.

The other concept is Stanley McChrystal's Law. The retired US Army general said, "It takes a network to defeat a network." His reference is to terrorist groups relating to national security, but the principle applies here as well. Successful inbound organizations will marshal the ecosystem's resources and lead their network of connections to successfully serve a set of customers and by extension everyone in their networks. Inbound organizations recognize that we are all connected, and no one can succeed alone.

Companies that participate in inbound ecosystems are frequently organized differently. They often feature loose connections, allowing for maximum flexibility and large amounts of autonomy. Traditional companies that haven't embraced inbound ecosystems tend to be hierarchical and bureaucratic, with set rules and procedures to make decisions.

If everyone's customers are already connected and part of a vast digitally enabled network, you can either support that network or ignore it.

Dan tells this story:

> *There are lots of times when I'll go visit a company that uses a competing software product, and I won't even mention Hub-Spot. I'll say, "I don't care what software you are using today. I'm here to help." Let me know your biggest inhibitors to growth, I am happy to offer my expertise and do the best I can to help you grow. Sooner or later, you might decide you want to improve your lead generation, customer acquisition, customer engagement, or competitive advantage and hopefully, you will remember my visit. I don't care if you buy software today, next week, or ever. What I'm looking to do is to establish the relationship so that if you are ever in that position, you will think of HubSpot first. When the time comes, when you raise your hand, BOOM. We will be ready to go.*

Are you helping as many people as you can? Do you have educational materials, videos, checklists, or white papers that would accelerate people's ability to solve problems if you made them available to everyone, for free? How would this information be perceived in your market, by your customers, and by prospects?

Todd is a member of a group of HubSpot partners called CoGrow, which acts as a peer group to share best practices and experiences. What makes this group unique is the founding idea behind it, which is to work together, to grow together, to make everyone in the group a better agency and better marketers. Also, to work together to grow the total audience for all of our services. One tactic the group uses is crowdsourcing content to attract more followers. Technically, all of the members are competitors, but that is not a barrier to sharing and working together. The ecosystem is far more valuable than the threat of aiding a potential competitor or losing business.

Building an inbound ecosystem also creates a barrier effect to your competition. The more interconnected relationships exist in an ecosystem, the more value for each member. Getting the members to align their visions, investments, and shared outcomes helps improve the relationship for everyone.

Inbound organizations apply most of the same principles of an inbound culture to the ecosystem. Transparency, putting people first, building autonomous teams, and making decisions close to the nodes in the ecosystem all apply.

Every organization exists within an ecosystem. Inbound organizations realize the power of helping everyone in that network. The simplest way to help everyone in your ecosystem is to help them grow their business.

Inbound ecosystems are not necessarily a profit center, but they are an investment in spreading the philosophy that can help your company grow. Everyone in the ecosystem must benefit, and as the ecosystem grows in size, the value for everyone grows accordingly.

Examples of adding value to your ecosystem include:

- Connecting buyers and sellers (like Cerasis in Chapter 10)
- Inspiring people to join a community with a strong mission and vision
- Sharing information or expertise around a particular problem
- Promoting speakers, books, and content to your audience
- Referring business to others
- Co-marketing with complimentary products or services
- Collaborating to create content and jointly promoting it
- Sharing your expertise with 3 and young entrepreneurs
- Creating a networking group of your skill set peers across industries

Inbound organizations nurture ecosystems as a natural extension of the inbound philosophy and culture. It requires a People First mindset and helping before selling.

To Do

☐ Evaluate current opportunities with in your existing communities.

☐ Evaluate the potential for creating and sustaining a unique industry ecosystem.

☐ Start small and build your ecosystem.

Chapter 28

The Inbound Organization in 10 Years

I s inbound really a revolution? It was started by a small group of passionate people that had a nearly impossible goal—to change the way small and midmarket companies marketed and sold and to help them grow. It introduced a very specific methodology that defined an innovative way to create a competitive advantage. It was supported by thousands of smaller businesses who were willing to take a risk by embracing unconventional thinking. It grew from a few early adopters to hundreds of practitioners, then thousands, and now millions.

There were numerous offshoots, iterations, updates, stops, and starts along the way. Lots of companies entered the ecosystem to connect, compete, and iterate. Inbound is now taught in hundreds of universities worldwide, with tens of thousands of certified professionals and thousands of certified partners. More and more companies are leveraging inbound for their culture, systems, and new business development process.

A dominant theme emerged in the first decade of inbound growth: regardless of your position, whether you decided to practice inbound or not, everyone was impacted in some way. Companies that embraced inbound, the philosophy and culture, inbound sales, and inbound marketing claimed a huge competitive advantage as the evolution of the modern buyer became mainstream. This advantage takes the form of visibility via website traffic and social media, lead generation capabilities, customers' engagement, and potentially high-value employees. Companies that decide to continue with traditional methods are also being impacted. As it becomes harder to generate new customers and more difficult to reach prospects, they watch as their customers get to choose from more options. Buyers are also affected as they realize how to leverage the code and content funnels to their advantage.

The future belongs to organizations that embrace inbound because buyers are not going back to a world where interruptive marketing rules the day.

There were two consistent responses from the experts we asked about the future of inbound.

One, tools and technology will continue to improve, allowing buyers more ease of use in research and organizations to understand buyers in more detail. Technology tools will help companies be more specific in understanding who prospects are, what prospects want, and where they are in the buyer journey. It will be even easier for inbound organizations to have more specific context, insight, and actionable information about buyers in a segment of one.

Two, both buyers and employees will continue to crave more human, helpful, and relevant experiences with the companies they choose. The core beliefs of inbound will become the minimum requirements in the future.

During the next phase of inbound, buyers will customize their interactions with sellers, rather than the other way around. Buyers will be able to create a buyer profile with personal and company information, preferences, habits, history, and goals. It might not even feel like a buyer/seller relationship. The "seller" will be available when the buyer is ready, with clear, helpful, useful information, and product and service combinations that will match their needs exactly. The buyer won't even have to look for it. The goal of one-to-one marketing will be much closer to reality.

"The future will be more individualized with highly customized relationships," is the way HubSpot's Andrew Quinn describes it.

Suneera Madhani of Fattmerchant describes her view of the future: "Buyers will expect things to be created with them in mind, more narrowly designed for them, more personal, and for sure delivered the right way, at the right time."[1]

Bob Ruffolo, owner of IMPACT, a company with a mission to help other businesses improve with inbound, puts it this way: "Technology is going to continue to improve the ability of companies to connect to more people who want a more personal level of service. If you have a product based or an internally based mindset, the distance between what you're doing and what people expect will dramatically increase."[2]

If businesses don't start adopting inbound principles and the buyer-centric mindset now, the technology gap will make those companies more and more irrelevant.

Technology Will Drive Marketing and Sales Personalization

Artificial intelligence (AI) will interact with marketers to plan, create, build, promote, and execute marketing campaigns.

Salesforce has acquired AI tools and integrated them into their CRM products. Marc Benioff, Salesforce CEO, says, "Put bluntly, if Einstein can find the best leads and set up an email prompt, what's to stop it from one day closing the deal itself?"[3]

Seventh Sense co-founder and CTO Erik LaBianca talks about AI and sales activities:

> *As things stand, salespeople and marketers routinely lose deals and customers by not following their process or not fully understanding their customer. AI is well-suited to*

tackle both of these problems, by tracking the buyer's journey and providing sales and marketing support, and by applying behavior data to segmentation and targeting instead of back-of-the-envelope guesses.

For instance, instead of relying on a checklist that probably doesn't exist or is ignored, AI could populate a profile for each incoming lead and select an appropriate call or email script to ensure that an inbound sales representative is able to articulate value in a way the customer can appreciate.

Or, instead of guessing how well a given piece of content will resonate with a target segment, AI can provide real-time feedback to the writer, suggesting possible changes to target a given interest segment, or providing a view of who is most likely to appreciate the piece.[4]

Paul Roetzer, founder and CEO of PR 20/20 and creator of the Marketing Artificial Intelligence Institute, adds: "If you make a list of all the things that inbound marketers do every day—from setting up automation rules to writing emails, to doing A/B testing, picking editorial calendar topics, scheduling social shares and keep going down the list—there isn't a single obstacle to intelligently automating any one of those tasks that enough money and time wouldn't get through."[5]

Dharmesh Shah on the future of bots:

One of the big reasons behind the consumer shift to messaging applications and live chat is the buyer preference for getting more immediate, real-time communication, completely on your own terms. Bots are really handy. They do a lot of routine tasks, they deliver accurate and effective information, and they can delight customers with a quick response. Which plays right into buyers' new expectation of response times and helps optimize which leads go where.

In addition, most people want a business to be available 24/7. This can seem daunting, particularly for smaller businesses and startups who may not have the resources to deploy an army of live representatives to look after a new channel where immediacy is key.

Bots give us the unique opportunity to seamlessly automate the conversations that users have with businesses in a highly personal and convenient way. With bots, people can chat with businesses immediately, regardless of where they are, what time zone they're in, or what their needs are. Bots do not get tired or overwhelmed; they do not grow impatient. Put simply: in this new, conversation-centric landscape, bots will give our customers an unfair advantage.[6]

AI and bots are two of the many technological changes we expect in the next decade. Technologies like virtual reality and blockchain will make further inroads into marketing.

Governments will almost certainly regulate large social media and Internet companies. Data privacy will continue to be a concern and a source of ongoing regulation. Regulation, however, will not stop the pace of new technology impacting the process of buying and selling.

The Inbound Organization in 10 Years

People will continue to seek out more human, helpful, and relevant experiences and continue to want to work for companies that align with their social goals. Adopting the core beliefs of inbound will become a natural part of any new business and will increasingly become the norm for all companies.

Here are some thoughts on the inbound organization in the next decade:

- ◆ Marketing moves to SMarketing with the elimination of the decades-old, archaic delineation between the two departments.
- ◆ Companies will post more content on central repository websites than on their own.

- Spending will continue to move away from interruption marketing to inbound initiatives.
- Customer-focused teams will collect better data and develop insights in a more natural way.
- Influencers and crowdsourcing of content will continue to grow including reviews, rankings, and comments from real buyers.
- More personal direct messaging with buyers.
- More intuitive search and social media tools will appear to help buyers understand how to start, evaluate, and decide all purchases.
- Customized options and concierge service will become more popular.
- Service interactions will become more immediate and seamless and built into the product or service.
- Organizations will create deeper and wider ecosystems to leverage the power of a network, collaborating to solve problems and add value for buyers.
- Organizations will monitor and adjust based on real-time feedback from equipment, service sites, websites, mobile phones, and any other customer connection point.

As buyer control continues to expand, marketing leaders will continue to exert more influence in organizations. Marketers will gain more clout within inbound organizations, all the way up to board of director positions. Executives with inbound marketing experience will rise to the top positions as more companies discover that customer-centricity must be reflected in all aspects of the management structure.

Customer-centric skills and expertise will be the key organizational characteristics. World-class companies will actively recruit employees with inbound skills.

Inbound organizations will continue to turn to distributed workforces to find talent and recruit more remote employees. One of the most common complaints of business leaders is the lack of talent available to fill digital marketing spots. To address this, companies will build networks of gig workers, part-time employees, and contract workers from wherever they can find them. New skills sharing platforms will arrive, allowing people to apply their skills to problems and for customers across a wider variety of industries and types of expertise. Physical location will continue to be less important than finding the person with the right skills.

Millennials will be moving into senior leadership positions within the next 10 years and will expect their businesses to be inbound with a corresponding culture. They will expect their companies to be transparent, socially conscious, diverse, sharing, and a fulfilling place to work. We expect the trend toward company culture as a competitive advantage to accelerate.

Adopt Inbound

The organizations that adopt inbound, gather the best buyer behavior data, understand how to derive insights from that data, and have a vision to leverage emerging technologies will be the winners in buyers' minds.

The companies that recognize and adopt inbound will be able to deliver amazing customer experiences. These companies will create differentiation, in some cases an insurmountable advantage, and establish first mover advantage in many, if not all, industries and market segments.

The organizations that understand these ideas now have the best chance to be the winners in the future.

Inbound values won't change in the future, but strategies, tactics, and processes will evolve. The following are some likely attributes of organizations in another decade:

- ♦ Organizations will be mission focused with a strong sense of social responsibility.
- ♦ Trust will be the currency of relationships.

- Business will be more human (even when you are working with bots).
- Radical transparency will be expected of everyone and in every relationship.
- Buyers will expect more personalization.
- Sellers will match engagement to the buyer's journey.
- Decisions will be made close to the customer by cross-functional teams.
- Employees will continue to expect to work with a purpose and a plan for advancement.
- Communication will be open and available when customers, partners, and employees want it.

Katie Burke describes her view of HubSpot and inbound in the future this way:

> *What inbound stands for will stay the same (relevance, humanity, and growth), but how it takes shape in terms of technology and products will change dramatically. My hope is that our philosophy stays the same but our product and platform evolve to meet the changing needs of our prospects and customers.*[7]

Dharmesh Shah summarizes the future of inbound:

> *Inbound principles will remain the same, but we will have evolved our practices. The idea of solving for the customer will be second-nature for many organizations. They will channel more and more of their marketing and sales investments to the things that drive the best ROI, namely, delighted customers that provide referrals. The technology will have evolved to allow companies to provide smooth, fluid ways for customers to engage. Everything will work from one shared understanding of the customer. This shared understanding will be used to personalize the experience, and the underlying data can power machine learning*

algorithms to go even further and make recommendations and predictions.[8]

Inbound has already become more than just a marketing strategy. The original strategy reflected the changes in buying behavior, but inbound today has come to represent a way of thinking, a mindset, and a philosophy for growing your business in the 21st century.

The world will become more inbound because people will become more inbound.

Buyers will crave ever more human treatment from companies; they will seek only helpful companies, not self-serving ones.

Human, helpful, relevant.

Inbound embodies these ideas. The future belongs to the inbound organization.

Notes

Preface

1. Erik Brynjolfsson and Andrew McAfee, *The Second Machine Age: Work, Progress, and Prosperity in a Time of Brilliant Technologies* (New York: W. W. Norton & Company, 2014).

Introduction

1. All quotations from Suneera Madhani used in the Introduction are from the following source: Suneera Madhani, phone interview with Todd Hockenberry, September 1, 2017.

2. All quotations from Liz Connett used in the Introduction are from the following source: Liz Connett, phone interview with Todd Hockenberry, September 29, 2017.

Chapter 1. Doing Business in the Twenty-First Century

1. Brian Hopkins, "Why You Are Getting Disrupted," Forrester, May 9, 2017, https://go.forrester.com/blogs/17-05-09-why_you_are_getting_disrupted/.

2. Ernest Hemingway, "Ernest Hemingway > Quotes > Quotable Quote," Goodreads, https://www.goodreads.com/quotes/102579-how-did-you-go-bankrupt-two-ways-gradually-then-suddenly.

3. BIA/Kelsey, "Nearly All Consumers (97%) Now Use Online Media to Shop Locally, According to BIA/Kelsey and ConStat," Cision PR Newswire, March 10, 2010, https://www.prnewswire.com/news-releases/nearly-all-consumers-97-now-use-online-media-to-shop-locally-according-to-biakelsey-and-constat-87221242.html.

4. Liz Smyth, "B2B Marketing in a Downturn Part 1: Lead Generation and Lead Nurturing," Marketo, March 2012, https://blog.marketo.com/2012/

03/b2b-marketing-in-a-downturn-part-1-lead-generation-and-nurture
.html.

5. Google, "Winning the Zero Moment of Truth," 2011, https://www
.thinkwithgoogle.com/_qs/documents/673/2011-winning-zmot-ebook
_research-studies.pdf.

6. Lori Wizdo, "Are Your Reps Butchering Your Early-Stage Leads?" Forrester, July 29, 2015, https://go.forrester.com/blogs/15-07-28-are_your_
reps_butchering_your_early_stage_leads/.

7. Ibid.

8. Kristina Jaramillo, "B2B Buyers Are Calling for a Change in How You
Socially Sell to Them on LinkedIn," Salesforce, April 20, 2016, https://www
.salesforce.com/blog/2016/04/b2b-buyers-change-social-sell-on-
linkedin.html.

9. Lori Wizdo, "Myth Busting 101: Insights into the B2B Buyer Journey,"
Forrester, May 25, 2015, https://go.forrester.com/blogs/15-05-25-
myth_busting_101_insights_intothe_b2b_buyer_journey/.

10. Erik Brynjolfsson and Andrew McAfee, *The Second Machine Age: Work,
Progress, and Prosperity in a Time of Brilliant Technologies* (New York:
W. W. Norton & Company, 2014).

Chapter 2. Buyer Expectations Have Changed

1. Marcus Sheridan, phone interview with Todd Hockenberry, April 6,
2017.

2. Michael Hammer and James Champy, *Reengineering the Corporation*
(New York: HarperCollins, 2003).

Chapter 3. The Building Blocks of an Inbound Organization

1. Andrea Miller, "Inbound Marketing Is Evolving—Are You Keeping Up?"
SproutContent, March 31, 2017, https://www.sproutcontent.com/blog/
inbound-marketing-is-evolving-are-you-keeping-up.

2. Kim Gittleson, "Can a Company Live Forever?," *BBC News*, January 19,
2012, http://www.bbc.com/news/business-16611040.

3. Vala Afshar, "50 Important Customer Experience Stats for Business Leaders," *HuffPost*, October 15, 2015, https://www.huffingtonpost .com/vala-afshar/50-important-customer-exp_b_8295772.html.

4. Jim Tierney, "Mercedes Benz CEO: Customer Experience Is the New Marketing," Loyalty360, October 8, 2014, https://loyalty360.org/content-gallery/daily-news/mercedes-benz-ceo-customer-experience-is-the-new-marketing.

5. Barbara Farfan, "Zappos CEO Tony Hsieh on Great Customer Service," *the balance*, July 13, 2017, https://www.thebalance.com/zappos-ceo-tony-hsieh-on-passion-2892515.

Chapter 4. Inbound Assessment and the MSPOT

1. Brian Halligan, "Scale-up Leadership Lessons I've Learned over 9 Years as HubSpot's CEO," thinkgrowth.org, January 10, 2016, https://thinkgrowth.org/scale-up-leadership-lessons-i-ve-learned-over-9-years-as-hubspot-s-ceo-39521f5b7567.

Chapter 5. Start with Your Mission

1. Simon Sinek, *Find Your Why: A Practical Guide for Discovering Purpose for You and Your Team* (New York: Portfolio/Penguin, 2017), 6.

2. Frank Auger, interview with Todd Hockenberry and Dan Tyre, November 16, 2017.

3. Stacey Ferreira, phone interview with Todd Hockenberry and Dan Tyre, December 8, 2017.

4. Amelia Wilcox, phone interview with Todd Hockenberry and Dan Tyre, November 28, 2017.

5. Bob Ruffolo, phone interview with Todd Hockenberry, January 23, 2018.

6. Dharmesh Shah, email exchange with Todd Hockenberry and Dan Tyre, December 1, 2017.

7. Ed Zitron, "Why Businesses That Are Purpose-Driven Come Out on Top," *Inc.*, April 9, 2015, https://www.inc.com/ed-zitron/why-businesses-that-are-purpose-come-out-on-top.html.

Chapter 6. Building a Culture That Reflects Inbound Values

1. J. D. Sherman, phone interview with Todd Hockenberry and Dan Tyre, November 13, 2017.

2. Dharmesh Shah, email exchange with Dan Tyre and Todd Hockenberry, December 1, 2017.

3. Patrick M. Lencioni, *The Advantage: Why Organizational Health Trumps Everything Else In Business* (San Francisco: Jossey-Bass, 2012).

4. Oscar Raymundo, "Richard Branson: Companies Should Put Employees First," *Inc.*, October 28, 2014, https://www.inc.com/oscar-raymundo/richard-branson-companies-should-put-employees-first.html.

5. Dharmesh Shah, email exchange with Dan Tyre and Todd Hockenberry, December 1, 2017.

6. Frank Auger, phone interview with Todd Hockenberry and Dan Tyre, November 16, 2017.

7. Eric Richard, "How We Gave SSL to All Our Customers in 5 Days for Free," HubSpot, November 16, 2017, http://product.hubspot.com/blog/how-we-gave-ssl-to-all-our-customers-in-5-days-for-free.

8. J. D. Sherman, phone interview with Todd Hockenberry and Dan Tyre, November 13, 2017.

9. Andrew Quinn, phone interview with Todd Hockenberry, October 10, 2017.

10. Dharmesh Shah, "What Elon Musk Taught Me about Growing a Business," thinkgrowth.org, October 16, 2017, https://thinkgrowth.org/what-elon-musk-taught-me-about-growing-a-business-c2c173f5bff3.

11. Brad Coffey, phone interview with Todd Hockenberry and Dan Tyre, November 16, 2017.

Chapter 7. Inbound Decision Making

1. Dharmesh Shah, "The "Optionality Tax" Is One of the Biggest Lessons We've Learned at HubSpot," *Medium*, February 26, 2016, https://medium.com/@dharmesh/the-optionality-tax-is-one-of-the-biggest-lessons-we-ve-learned-at-hubspot-5572ce497877.

2. Sam Mallikarjunan, "The Difference Between Internal Disruption and Uninspired Optionality," thinkgrowth.org, November 14, 2017, https://

thinkgrowth.org/the-difference-between-internal-disruption-and-uninspired-optionality-fd2596ee45e3.

3. J. D. Sherman, phone interview with Todd Hockenberry and Dan Tyre, November 13, 2017.

4. Brian Halligan, "Scale-up Leadership Lessons I've Learned over 9 Years as HubSpot's CEO," thinkgrowth.org, January 10, 2016, https://thinkgrowth.org/scale-up-leadership-lessons-i-ve-learned-over-9-years-as-hubspot-s-ceo-39521f5b7567.

5. J. D. Sherman, phone interview with Todd Hockenberry and Dan Tyre, November 13, 2017.

6. Brad Coffey, phone interview with Todd Hockenberry and Dan Tyre, November 16, 2017.

Chapter 8. Create an Inbound Operating System

1. J. D. Sherman, phone interview with Todd Hockenberry and Dan Tyre, November 13, 2017.

2. Dharmesh Shah, "The HubSpot Culture Code: Creating a Company We Love," March 23, 2013, https://cdn2.hubspot.net/hub/216938/file-24940534-pdf/docs/culturecode-v7–130320111259-phpapp02.pdf.

3. Dharmesh Shah, email exchange with Todd Hockenberry and Dan Tyre, December 1, 2017.

4. Andrew Mahon, interview with Todd Hockenberry, September 26, 2017.

5. Bob Ruffolo, phone interview with Todd Hockenberry, January 23, 2018.

6. Natalie Davis, phone interview with Todd Hockenberry, January 23, 2018.

7. J. D. Sherman, phone interview with Todd Hockenberry and Dan Tyre, November 13, 2017.

Chapter 9. Find Inbound People

1. Hannah Fleishman, phone interview with Todd Hockenberry, September 13, 2017.

2. Deloitte, "The Deloitte Millennial Survey 2017," Deloitte, January 31, 2017, https://www2.deloitte.com/global/en/pages/about-deloitte/articles/millennialsurvey.html.

3. M. Tarpey, "76% of Candidates Want to Know about Day-to-Day Responsibilities," CareerBuilder, June 13, 2016, https://resources.careerbuilder.com/recruiting-solutions/define-candidate-responsibilities.

4. Paul Roetzer, phone interview with Todd Hockenberry, November 20, 2017.

5. Hannah Fleischman, phone interview with Todd Hockenberry, September 13, 2017.

6. Ibid.

7. Mike Ewing, phone interview with Todd Hockenberry, March 3, 2017.

8. Dharmesh Shah, "The HubSpot Culture Code: Creating a Company We Love," March 23, 2013, https://cdn2.hubspot.net/hub/216938/file-24940534-pdf/docs/culturecode-v7–130320111259-phpapp02.pdf.

9. Katie Burke, "The Path to Making People a Priority," thinkgrowth.org, January 31, 2017, https://thinkgrowth.org/the-path-to-making-people-a-priority-4fbb1f181b8c.

10. Dharmesh Shah, email exchange with Todd Hockenberry and Dan Tyre, December 1, 2017.

Chapter 10. Cerasis—Culture Creating a Movement Around a Mission

*All quotations from Adam Robinson used in Chapter 10 are from the following source: Adam Robinson, interview with Todd Hockenberry, August 14, 2017.

Chapter 11. Inbound Strategies—Change from Selling to Helping People

1. Dharmesh Shah, email exchange with Todd Hockenberry and Dan Tyre, December 1, 2017.

2. Robert B. Cialdini, *Influence: The Psychology of Persuasion* (New York: William Morrow and Company, 1993).

3. Kristina Jaramillo, "B2B Buyers Are Calling for a Change in How You Socially Sell to Them on LinkedIn," *Salesforce*, April 20, 2016, https://www.salesforce.com/blog/2016/04/b2b-buyers-change-social-sell-on-linkedin.html.

4. Rachel Leist, phone interview with Todd Hockenberry, August 7, 2017.

5. Clayton Christensen, Scott Cook, and Taddy Hall, January 16, 2006, https://hbswk.hbs.edu/item/what-customers-want-from-your-products.

6. Clayton M. Christensen, Taddy Hall, Karen Dillon, and David S. Duncan, "Know Your Customers' 'Jobs to Be Done,'" *Harvard Business Review*, September 1, 2016, https://hbr.org/2016/09/know-your-customers-jobs-to-be-done.

7. Food Marketing Institute, "Honest Clarity Is the Next Food Retail Strategy," June 12, 2107, https://www.fmi.org/newsroom/news-archive/view/2017/06/12/honest-clarity-is-the-next-food-retail-strategy.

Chapter 12. Inbound Strategies Are Engagement Focused

1. Erik Brynjolfsson and Andrew McAfee, *The Second Machine Age: Work, Progress, and Prosperity in a Time of Brilliant Technologies* (New York: W. W. Norton, 2014).

2. Seth Godin, "When in Doubt, Connect," *Seth's Blog*, August 6, 2017, http://sethgodin.typepad.com/seths_blog/2017/08/when-in-doubt-connect.html.

3. Brian Halligan, "Doing Business With 'Why'," *Inc.*, July 24, 2014, https://www.inc.com/brian-halligan/doing-business-with-8220-why-8221.html.

4. Alan Zorfas and Daniel Leemon, "An Emotional Connection Matters More than Customer Satisfaction," *Harvard Business Review*, August 29, 2016, https://hbr.org/2016/08/an-emotional-connection-matters-more-than-customer-satisfaction.

5. Courtney Sembler, "Personalizing Your Conversations in Sales and Marketing," HubSpot, July 27, 2017, https://blog.hubspot.com/customers/personalizing-conversations-sales-marketing.

6. Jess Marranco, "Human-to-Human Marketing: A Trend for 2015 and Beyond," HubSpot, December 17, 2014, https://blog.hubspot.com/marketing/human-to-human-marketing.

7. "Facebook Messenger Day Hits 70M Daily Users as the App Reaches 1.3B Monthlies," TechCrunch, 14 September 2017, https://techcrunch.com/2017/09/14/facebook-messenger-1-3-billion.

8. Alex Debecker, "3 Stats That Show Chatbots Are Here to Stay," VentureBeat, August 26, 2016, https://venturebeat.com/2016/08/26/3-stats-that-show-chatbots-are-here-to-stay/.

9. Ibid.

10. Mimi An, "Buyers Speak Out: How Sales Needs to Evolve," HubSpot, April 7, 2016, https://research.hubspot.com/reports/buyers-speak-out-how-sales-needs-to-evolve.

Chapter 13. Inbound Strategies Are Persona Based

1. Clayton M. Christensen, Taddy Hall, Karen Dillon, and David S. Duncan, "Know Your Customers' 'Jobs to Be Done,'" *Harvard Business Review*, September 1, 2016, https://hbr.org/2016/09/know-your-customers-jobs-to-be-done.

2. Marcus Sheridan, phone interview with Todd Hockenberry, April 6, 2017.

3. Bob Thompson, May 28, 2016 "Take a Tip from Bezos: Customers Always Need a Seat at the Table," https://www.entrepreneur.com/article/234254.

4. Adele Revella, phone interview with Todd Hockenberry, September 1, 2017.

5. Adele Revella, *Buyer Personas: How to Gain Insight into Your Customer's Expectations, Align Your Marketing Strategies, and Win More Business* (Hoboken, NJ: John Wiley & Sons, 2015).

6. Adele Revella, phone interview with Todd Hockenberry, September 1, 2017.

Chapter 15. Inbound Strategies Match the Buyer's Journey

1. Stephen R. Covey, *The 7 Habits of Highly Effective People* (New York: Fireside, 1990).

2. Adam Robinson, phone interview with Todd Hockenberry, August 14, 2017.

3. Rachel Leist, phone interview with Todd Hockenberry, August 7, 2017.

4. N. J. Webb, *What Customers Crave: How to Create Relevant and Memorable Experiences at Every Touchpoint* (New York: AMACOM, 2017).

5. Kristina Jaramillo, "B2B Buyers Are Calling for a Change in How You Socially Sell to Them on LinkedIn," Salesforce, April 20, 2016, https://

www.salesforce.com/blog/2016/04/b2b-buyers-change-social-sell-on-linkedin.html.

6. Google, "Winning the Zero Moment of Truth," 2011, https://www.thinkwithgoogle.com/_qs/documents/673/2011-winning-zmot-ebook_research-studies.pdf.

7. BIA/Kelsey, "Nearly All Consumers (97%) Now Use Online Media to Shop Locally, According to BIA/Kelsey and ConStat," Cision PR Newswire, March 10, 2010, https://www.prnewswire.com/news-releases/nearly-all-consumers-97-now-use-online-media-to-shop-locally-according-to-biakelsey-and-constat-87221242.html.

Chapter 16. Centralized View of the Customer

1. Pete Caputa, phone interview with Todd Hockenberry, October 5, 2017.

2. Emma Brudner, "10 Major Benefits of CRM Systems (Infographic)," HubSpot, April 5, 2016, https://blog.hubspot.com/sales/benefits-crm-system-infographic.

Chapter 18. Inbound Marketing Is a Strategic Imperative

1. BIA/Kelsey, "Nearly All Consumers (97%) Now Use Online Media to Shop Locally, According to BIA/Kelsey and ConStat," Cision PR Newswire, March 10, 2010, https://www.prnewswire.com/news-releases/nearly-all-consumers-97-now-use-online-media-to-shop-locally-according-to-biakelsey-and-constat-87221242.html.

2. Liz Smyth, "B2B Marketing in a Downturn Part 1: Lead Generation and Lead Nurturing," Marketo, March 2012, https://blog.marketo.com/2012/03/b2b-marketing-in-a-downturn-part-1-lead-generation-and-nurture.html.

3. Adam Robinson, phone interview with Todd Hockenberry, August 14, 2017.

4. D. McCullough, "David McCullough > Quotes > Quotable Quote," Goodreads, https://www.goodreads.com/quotes/320581-writing-is-thinking-to-write-well-is-to-think-clearly.

5. Janessa Lantz, interview with Todd Hockenberry, September 21, 2017.

6. Andrew Quinn, interview with Todd Hockenberry, October 10, 2017.

7. Janessa Lantz, interview with Todd Hockenberry, September 21, 2017.

8. Content Marketing Institute, "B2B Content Marketing: 2016 Benchmarks, Budgets, and Trends—North America," September 29, 2015, http://contentmarketinginstitute.com/wp-content/uploads/2015/09/2016_B2B_Report_Final.pdf.

9. Justin Champion, *Inbound Content: A Step-By-Step Guide to Doing Content Marketing the Inbound Way*, April 16, 2018, http://pdfmedia.co/36870420/inbound-content-a-step-by-step-guide-to-doing-content-marketing-the-inbound-way.html.

Chapter 19. Bell Performance—Content Attracting, Engaging, and Helping an Audience

1. Glenn Williams, phone interview with Todd Hockenberry, September 29, 2017.

2. Erik Bjornstad, phone interview with Todd Hockenberry, September 29, 2017.

3. Ibid.

4. Glenn Williams, phone interview with Todd Hockenberry, September 29, 2017.

5. Ibid.

Chapter 20. Inbound Selling

1. Dan Tyre, "Always Be Closing Is Dead: How to Always Be Helping in 2017," HubSpot, January 10, 2015, https://blog.hubspot.com/sales/always-be-closing-is-dead-how-to-always-be-helping-in-2015.

2. Brian Signorelli, email exchange with Todd Hockenberry and Dan Tyre, December 6, 2017.

Chapter 21. Yokel Local's Strange Trip to Becoming a HubSpot Agency Partner

1. Stormie Andrews and Darrell Evans, phone interview with Todd Hockenberry and Dan Tyre, October 26, 2017.

2. David Weinhaus, interview with Todd Hockenberry and Dan Tyre, December 6, 2017.

3. Ibid.

4. Ibid.

5. Ibid.

6. Stormie Andrews and Darrell Evans, phone interview with Todd Hockenberry and Dan Tyre, October 26, 2017.

7. David Weinhaus, interview with Todd Hockenberry and Dan Tyre, October 6, 2017.

8. Stormie Andrews and Darrell Evans, phone interview with Todd Hockenberry and Dan Tyre, October 26, 2017.

9. Ibid.

10. David Weinhaus, interview with Todd Hockenberry and Dan Tyre, October 6, 2017.

Chapter 22. SMarketing

1. Jeremy Miller, "Creating a First Call Advantage: Applying the 3% Rule," Sticky Branding, April 26, 2010, https://stickybranding.com/creating-a-first-call-advantage-applying-the-3-rule/.

2. Andrew Moravick, "Sales and Marketing Alignment: A Primer on Successful Collaboration," Aberdeen, July 13, 2017, http://aberdeen.com/research/8803/rb-sales-marketing-alignment-collaboration/content.aspx.

3. Brian Signorelli, email exchange with Todd Hockenberry and Dan Tyre, December 6, 2017.

4. HubSpot, "State of Inbound 2017," May 17, 2017, https://cdn2.hubspot.net/hubfs/53/assets/soi/2017/global/State%20of%20Inbound%202017.pdf.

Chapter 23. Tube Form Solutions—Aligning the Sales Team with Buyers

*All quotations by Mike Thomas used in Chapter 23 are from the following source: Mike Thomas, phone interview with Todd Hockenberry, September 29, 2017.

Chapter 24. Inbound Service

1. Matthew Dixon, Karen Freeman, and Nicholas Toman, "Stop Trying to Delight Your Customers," *Harvard Business Review*, July 1, 2010, https://hbr.org/2010/07/stop-trying-to-delight-your-customers.

2. Robert Wollan, Phil Davis, Fabio De Angelis, and Kevin Quiring, "Seeing Beyond the Loyalty Illusion: It's Time You Invest More Wisely," Accenture Strategy, February 16, 2017, https://www.accenture.com/t20170216T035010__w__/us-en/_acnmedia/PDF-43/Accenture-Strategy-GCPR-Customer-Loyalty.pdf.

3. Nate Munger, "Day Zero: A New Way to Define Customer Success," Intercom, November 11, 2016, https://blog.intercom.com/day-zero-a-new-way-to-define-customer-success/.

Chapter 25. Measuring the Health of Your Relationships

1. Michael Ewing, interview with Todd Hockenberry, March 3, 2017.
2. Michael Redbord, interview with Todd Hockenberry, August 7, 2017.

Chapter 26. Inbound Back Office

1. Erik Brynjolfsson and Andrew McAfee, *The Second Machine Age: Work, Progress, and Prosperity in a Time of Brilliant Technologies* (New York: W. W. Norton, 2014).

2. Michael Ewing, interview with Todd Hockenberry, March 3, 2017.

3. John Kelleher, interview with Todd Hockenberry and Dan Tyre, October 26, 2017.

4. Frank Auger, interview with Todd Hockenberry and Dan Tyre, November 16, 2017.

5. John Kelleher, interview with Todd Hockenberry and Dan Tyre, October 26, 2017.

Chapter 28. The Inbound Organization in 10 Years

1. Suneera Madhani, phone interview with Todd Hockenberry, September 1, 2017.

2. Bob Ruffolo, phone interview with Todd Hockenberry, October 20, 2017.

3. Marco della Cava, "Salesforce Unveils Einstein AI to Help Close Deals," *USA Today*, September 18, 2016, https://www.usatoday.com/story/tech/news/2016/09/18/salesforce-uses-ai-help-customers-close-deals/90506060/.

4. Paul Roetzer, "Seventh Sense Uses Artificial Intelligence to Optimize Email Send Times and Drive Engagement," Marketing Artificial Intelligence Institute, October 5, 2017, https://www.marketingaiinstitute.com/blog/seventh-sense-uses-artificial-intelligence-to-optimize-email-send-times-and-drive-engagement.

5. Paul Roetzer, phone interview with Todd Hockenberry, November 20, 2017.

6. Dharmesh Shah, email exchange wtih Todd Hockenberry and Dan Tyre, December 1, 2017.

7. Katie Burke, email exchange wtih Todd Hockenberry and Dan Tyre, October 14, 2017.

8. Dharmesh Shah, email exchange wtih Todd Hockenberry and Dan Tyre, December 1, 2017.

Index

Page numbers followed by *f* refer to figures.